Race and the Rhetoric of Resistance

Race and the Rhetoric of Resistance

JEFFREY B. FERGUSON

EDITED WITH A FOREWORD BY
WERNER SOLLORS

AFTERWORD BY
GEORGE B. HUTCHINSON

Rutgers University Press
New Brunswick, Camden, and Newark, New Jersey, and London

Library of Congress Cataloging-in-Publication Data
Names: Ferguson, Jeffrey B., 1964-2018, author. | Sollors, Werner, editor, writer of foreword. | Hutchinson, George, 1953- writer of afterword.
Title: Race and the rhetoric of resistance / by Jeffrey B. Ferguson ; edited and foreword by Werner Sollors ; afterword by George B. Hutchinson.
Description: New Brunswick, New Jersey : Rutgers University Press, [2021] | Includes bibliographical references and index.
Identifiers: LCCN 2020027847 | ISBN 9781978820838 (hardcover) | ISBN 9781978820821 (paperback) | ISBN 9781978820845 (epub) | ISBN 9781978820852 (mobi) | ISBN 9781978820869 (pdf)
Subjects: LCSH: African Americans—Historiography. | African Americans—Study and teaching—United States. | American literature—African American authors—History and criticism. | United States—Race relations—Historiography.
Classification: LCC E184.65 .F47 2021 | DDC 973/.04960730072—dc23
LC record available at https://lccn.loc.gov/2020027847

A British Cataloging-in-Publication record for this book is available from the British Library.

For permissions credits, please refer to the Editor's Acknowledgments.

∞ The paper used in this publication meets the requirements of the American National Standard for Information Sciences—Permanence of Paper for Printed Library Materials, ANSI Z39.48-1992.

www.rutgersuniversitypress.org

Manufactured in the United States of America

For Agustina, Django, and Ted

Contents

Foreword

WERNER SOLLORS

Jeffrey B. Ferguson, remembered as an Amherst College professor of mythical charisma and as the smart editor of the sourcebook *The Harlem Renaissance: A Brief History with Documents*, is best known for his long-standing engagement with the iconoclastic satirist George Schuyler. *The Sage of Sugar Hill: George S. Schuyler and the Harlem Renaissance* was a magnificent, meticulously researched, and paradigm-changing book, putting Schuyler at the very center of American and African American Studies. It forced the reader to take a fresh look at Schuyler's essays, his *Pittsburgh Courier* columns, and his novel *Black No More* and to question the lens of "race melodrama" through which so much American cultural history and storytelling has been filtered. Ferguson was attracted to Schuyler's "uncompromising skepticism" and to his sharp recognition of the "ludicrous and outlandish in American race relations." As Ferguson put it, in all the books he had read, "nothing came close to the irreverent force of Schuyler's satire." That irreverent force revealed the absurdities of the Jim Crow regime, under which "blacks felt themselves vulnerable to the desires of even the sickest whites." But Schuyler's satire, Ferguson argued convincingly and cogently, also reveals the absurdities of much thinking that has gone into "solving" the "race problem."

What would thinking about "race relations" be like if Schuyler's relentless questioning were heeded? How could the "bifurcating effects" of racial melodrama, the common, popular, and well-intentioned forms of sentimental heroization and victimization, be avoided in literary and in scholarly narratives?

Contemplation of such questions led Ferguson to the present more general new project, *Race and the Rhetoric of Resistance*, a critical examination of the fixtures of popular and scholarly discourse about blacks. Black Studies started out with a goal of correcting the clichés and omissions of American Studies. Ferguson takes this process one step further in also examining the often unquestioned clichés and commonplaces in African American Studies. The manifesto-like opening essay stakes his claims: "The broad and diverse discourse on African Americans has yielded many books, but only two basic stories: those of suffering and resistance. Whether through exaggeration, understatement, denial, or intricate combination, all others derive from these two." The lens immediately widens onto broader questions that should undergird any notions of suffering and resistance: "Can meaning or wisdom come from suffering? Or is suffering the permanent enemy of the free life? Does suffering contain its own transcendence? Or can it be justified only as means to the attainment of tangible worldly goods such as money, status, or political power?"

In "Freedom, Equality, Race," he questions the progressive mode in the many "from / to" narratives that abound in scholarship and commentary: from slavery to freedom and equality, from racial thinking to the expectation that racial distinctions would soon disappear. He notes the paradox that the Enlightenment "handed down most of the reasons to believe in race along with the justifications for despising and resisting it." And he endorses Nathan Huggins's assessment that what is needed, yet difficult to arrive at, is a "new narrative." In "A Blue Note on Black American Literary Criticism and the Blues" he takes a critical and deeply ironic view of the blues when understood as a cultural "matrix" for black literature and a site for resistance. Drawing on Albert Murray and Kenneth Burke, he instead finds that "the blues does not so much complain about the events of this life as it reports them, but in an artistic form that privileges improvisation and the potential for creative endeavor to reshape emotion." And "for the sake of sheer fun" he quotes lavishly and interprets blues texts like Lucille Bogan's "Shave 'Em Dry" that would seem to challenge conventional wisdom. In his lecture "Of Mr. W.E.B. Du Bois and Others" he distills various features of Du Bois's lasting legacy only to note, in contrasting Du Bois and Mahatma Gandhi, that Du Bois "needed to conceive of the slave, and of his segregated and much abused descendants, ultimately as contenders for power in order to imagine them achieving a place of honor and dignity in American society." What Ferguson found missing in this conception was "the sincere admission of vulnerability" that "stands behind the deepest human strength."

Ferguson goes deeper than any other literary or cultural critic in teasing out the ironies that have surrounded notions of race and racial cultural production in America. One further irony is that in order to highlight some of the past and current conundrums and blind spots of thinking about race, he draws on classic American Studies concepts and texts, including Ralph Waldo Emerson's distinction between the party of memory and the party of hope, Alexis de Tocqueville's notions of American democracy and the races of

America, Lionel Trilling's distinction between sincerity and authenticity, and Edmund Morgan's demonstration of the interconnectedness of American slavery and American freedom. Furthermore, Ferguson offers a path toward a philosophical understanding of the race complex and the human condition by drawing on Rousseau and Nietzsche, Hannah Arendt and Tzvetan Todorov, as well as on Max Scheler's notion of ressentiment. Thus he can detect in major works in the African American tradition what he calls the "broad boulevard of Western thought."

Elegant and often aphoristic, these memorable essays amount to a serious, principled critique of common popular and scholarly notions of racial difference. They also convey their author's sense of humor, warmth, and grace. He completed them between 2008 and 2013, but they resonate at a later time when race has once again taken on a crucial urgency in American life. Ferguson meant to complement these chapters by additional work, of which "Notes on Escape" is an unfinished example. He hoped to address other "major manifestations of resistant thought and activity in African American history," including violence, transgression, and subversion. And he planned an epilogue that would "reach for a deeper synthesis of the book's main themes, involving tragedy, vulnerability, and freedom." Sketching the broader vision he had for the whole undertaking, he wrote compellingly: "More than strength, human beings have common cause in our weakness, susceptibility, and mutual dependence. Ethics begins with the condition of the slave, the prisoner, the peon, and with the one who suffers for no reason. The only resistance worth supporting is the one that reduces the salience of force in our lives, not the one that celebrates it." His long illness, which he valiantly fought and to which he succumbed on March 11, 2018, prevented him from completing this project, yet as George Hutchinson shows in the afterword to this volume, "the essays collected here form a coherent argument." Jeffrey B. Ferguson's *Race and the Rhetoric of Resistance* is the result of critical thinking by a truly free mind, and it is hoped that this book will inspire others to engage with and to extend the work that he started.

Race and the Rhetoric of Resistance

Race and the Rhetoric of Resistance

The broad and diverse discourse on African Americans has yielded many books, but only two basic stories: those of suffering and resistance. Whether through exaggeration, understatement, denial, or intricate combination, all others derive from these two. Stated directly, the issues around these two stories seem more properly philosophical than historical or political, although they relate to every level of African American life, including the most intimate and personal. Like all such piercing matters, they also go beyond specifically racial concerns to ancient and interminable questions regarding the fundamental capacities of beings such as ourselves. Can meaning or wisdom come from suffering? Or is suffering the permanent enemy of the free life? Does suffering contain its own transcendence? Or can it be justified only as a means to the attainment of tangible worldly goods such as money, status, or political power? Such concerns have informed the race question as they have directed the general thrust of modern life. Animated in part by a stubborn faith in the human ability to resist or eliminate suffering through self-invention, technology, political movement, economic production, and many other means, modern societies have nonetheless remade human torment along myriad lines. As a leading concept of modernity, as a multiform social and political reality, and as lived experience, race has stood out for the extreme way that it manifests both the persistence of suffering and the great hope that by fighting against it human beings might deliver themselves from its grasp.

The African American circumstance of exile, enslavement, segregation, and natal alienation has led naturally to a deep contemplation of the relationship between suffering and resistance, but it has yielded no sure answers. One influential side of the tradition regards suffering as a key to insight and creativity, while another regards it as an unequivocal negative, something to be fought, escaped, and constantly resisted. W.E.B. Du Bois had something like the former in mind when he spoke of African American "second sight" or of the wisdom of the sorrow songs in *The Souls of Black Folk*. So did Janie in Zora Neale Hurston's *Their Eyes Were Watching God*, when she said to her "kissin friend" Pheoby, "You got to go there to know there two things everybody got to do for theyselves. They got to go to God, and they got to find out about living." In order to achieve her inner victory, and in the end to pull in her horizon "from around the waist of the world" "like a great fishnet" with "life in its meshes," Janie had to suffer tremendous loss. Without this, her act of self-possession in telling her own story in her own way could not have occurred. Something similar might be said of the blues singer Ma Rainey from Sterling Brown's poem of the same name, who drew crowds from all around by singing about hard luck and "'bout de lonesome road / We mus' go"; or of Ralph Ellison's nameless protagonist in *Invisible Man*, who learned to see the good air that danced from the visible end of Louis Armstrong's trumpet as the product of the more essential, sweaty, spittle-laced bad air on the business end. His marijuana-induced descent through the invisible levels of Armstrong's unforgettable song "Black and

Blue" foreshadows a painful journey where he learns, like Hurston's Janie, that genuine life stories, black or otherwise, are always expensive.

With a similar aim in mind, but in a register more informed by the African American Christian tradition than by the blues, James Baldwin in *The Fire Next Time* relates the tragic bottom line of race relations to his nephew: that in order to love himself fully, he must love whites, however much they hate him. If he can do this, Baldwin says, he will have paid the price to possess the wisdom of his slave ancestors, who understood the redemptive value of undeserved suffering. Praising the poetry of the ancestors, Baldwin quotes a poignant line from the spirituals as his argumentative coup de grâce: "At the very time I thought I was lost, my dungeon shook, and my chains fell off." In other words, when one reaches the lowest and most wretched depths of existence, one depends most on faith. There, facing the chaos but aligned with God, the weakest man becomes the strongest. He may be physically chained, but spiritually and mentally he has achieved freedom in the deepest sense. In *Black Odyssey*, the historian Nathan Huggins seizes the same idea in order to cast the African American slave as a stoic whose sure apprehension of humanity under American tyranny provides the most viable alternative to the hegemonic force of progressive ideology, the dominant value in the master narrative of American history. According to Huggins, in order to preserve this grand narrative, American historians have depicted slavery and the subsequent events of the African American past as aberrations within a national story of expanding freedom, abundance, and democracy. Against this twice-told tale, he insists that American history began in tyranny, driven in part by the very progressive ideology that made the myth of American freedom and the reality of American slavery possible. Thus, he concludes that the decidedly unprogressive story of the dark and excluded, of human beings regarded as objects but with a keen sense of their human value, holds the key to a more inclusive, and more just, American national narrative.

Looked at one way, Huggins's call for a new American metanarrative squares well with ideas of resistance. The very gesture of the slave claiming her humanity contains within it an undeniable "no" to the slave owner, however much it says "yes" to God, to faith, or even to suffering. The same holds for the conceptions of black dignity through suffering articulated by Du Bois, Hurston's Janie, Baldwin, and others. Yet none of these figures puts forth resistance as *the* fundamental value. In *Black Odyssey*, Huggins emphasizes the maintenance of African American community and family against the dangers represented by rebels who sought escape or violent revenge. Huggins put the 1960s and 1970s romance of resistance in his crosshairs, insisting that the lasting meaning of slavery required recognizing that the inconvenient ironies of everyday human interaction exist in a tragic context of oppression. We might join him in doubting whether a theme like resistance, which focuses more on the struggle against outside forces than on inner experiences, can give the best account of how both oppressed and oppressor exceed the frameworks that we use to explain them.

Yet as we acknowledge Huggins's suspicions concerning the theme of resistance, we should also note that changes in the discourse on African Americans (and in American history in general) since the 1970s make some of his most important claims seem somewhat dated. However rooted in tragedy and irony, his ideas about African American dignity depend on notions of universal humanity that have long since fallen into disrepute, although it remains a puzzle how we might ground a concept like *dignity* without some idea of human commonality. Today, the standard perspective in the field emphasizes irreducible difference, incommensurability, and incongruity to such a degree that new grand narratives hardly seem possible, or even desirable. We think in parts, not wholes. Global contexts make Huggins's concern with American ideas of nationhood appear passé, even if our government's wasteful application of muscle-flexing, market-glorifying, neoliberal policies at home and abroad does legitimate his disdain for the ideology of progress. Huggins's tendency to describe slavery, and slaves, in overarching terms also runs against current sensibilities. And even if we could put aside the current preference for nonunitary accounts of slavery, slave stoicism might not strike us as the most usable inheritance. How many of us could embrace such an ideal, anyway? Looking back at slavery and at African American history in general from the current vantage point, we prefer to see our own situation more or less projected backward—where multiple identities, political power play, and social performance on fractured terrain form the order of the day. Yet, because of this, and despite all of the good reasons for rejecting major parts of his viewpoint, we might still pay attention to Huggins's call for a new story.

For the skeptic, the utter dominance of the theme of resistance in the current discourse on black Americans should evoke some suspicion. Almost everyone knows the fundamental contours of the resistance theme in one way or another because it has dominated both the popular and the scholarly discourses about blacks since the 1960s. In its popular guise, resistance usually appears as a story of heroic opposition in the face of oppression—as in the movies *The Jackie Robinson Story*, *The Tuskegee Airmen*, *Glory*, *Sweet Sweetback's Baadasssss Song*, or *Do the Right Thing*—but it also serves as the underlying paradigmatic inspiration for a wide range of representations, from James Brown's "Say It Out Loud" to "Fight the Power" by Public Enemy, to modes of self-fashioning among today's "gangsta rappers." The resistance theme also frames popular political symbolism from Martin Luther King Day to the Million Man March, as it plays a central role in current scholarship about black Americans. One can barely turn a few pages of a journal in the field of African American Studies without encountering an article focusing on the way some text, character, author, or figure in history has in one way or another stood against or slipped the yoke of material or ideological oppression. Quite often in these articles, resistance serves more as a rhetorical deal-closer than as an analytical concept, more of an answer that ends or suspends the conversation than as a problem that opens it to new territory.

Resistance is a constant theme of the historiography of slavery, of black literature and cultural theory, and of social scientific theories of black subjectivity and collective life. It practically defines Cultural Studies and Critical Race Studies, as well as the long Marxist tradition in the analysis of race relations going back to the 1910s. It also dominates the periodization of black American history. For example, we study the black migration and the Harlem Renaissance mainly for their resistance value. The Jim Crow period stands out as the opposite, as a time when black resistance and progress were beaten into submission. Yet prizewinning studies such as *Gender and Jim Crow* by Glenda Gilmore and *A Nation under Our Feet* by Steven Hahn reassure us that even here, in the darkest and most submissive period of postbellum black American history, resistance thrived. We may also owe the most commonly accepted name for our own period, the post–civil rights era, to the centrality of the resistance theme. If black American history is generally characterized as a progression from slavery to a culminating crescendo of resistance in the 1960s, it may not be a surprise that we have trouble imagining what comes after as anything but a "post." Under such conditions, it makes sense to wonder if the "post" will not go on indefinitely.

Resistance has always played an important role in the African American imagination, but only in the past decades has it become an indispensable tool of race interpretation. No doubt, the very first slave pondered resistance, as did his or her many descendants. Still, under conditions where rebellion stood a small chance of success and involved great risk to life, limb, and family, sane African Americans necessarily focused on other aspects of life, aspects that we miss in giving resistance too much weight. Contemplating the ethical circumstances of Holocaust victims and others under extreme forms of oppression in *Facing the Extreme*, Tzvetan Todorov theorizes that the victims of overwhelming power most often turn to serving the immediate human needs of the others around them rather than rushing heroically into the cannons and bayonets of the enemy. Here an ethics of care, the sustaining value of collective life, comes to the forefront. Focusing on the basic needs of wives, husbands, children, grandparents, and friends, he says, many Holocaust victims went quietly to their graves without raising a fist to their oppressors; yet they met their demise having served themselves and others more powerfully than they could have as pugnacious underdogs "pressed to the wall, but fighting back" (to borrow a phrase from Claude McKay). I cite Todorov here not to put forth his perspective as the only truth about men and women under conditions of extreme oppression, but only to point up a theme that our current emphasis on resistance tends to preclude. Like most dominant paradigms or "master narratives," the resistance framework obscures as much as it clarifies. While it emphasizes important aspects of African American life, including bravery, sacrifice, and ideas of dignity based on these, it tends to subsume such other themes as pleasure, artistic invention, religious belief, and issues of interracial and intraracial solidarity into a narrow set of dualities concerning submission and defiance. Sometimes the focus on resistance inspires an all too pat and unified picture of black life. And, at its worst, the resistance framework promotes a melodramatic logic of perpetrators and victims, or of righteous freedom fighters and evil masters.

While most recent, some might say "postmodern," approaches to African American resistance employ more sophisticated or ironic terms than these, almost all of them tend to follow a totalizing logic that sees resistance as the fundamental condition of black existence. Some studies of this type manage to find resistance of one sort or another in nearly every aspect of black American culture and social organization, but in such small and subtle quantities that they appear to make very little difference. Often, this comes dangerously close to finding resistance nowhere at all. Yet, despite all of my complaints about the resistance paradigm, I want not so much to argue against it as to explore the intellectual roots of our tremendous respect for it. Why, I wonder, have we come to connect race and resistance so insistently? What ideas do we find at the core of this concern?

As an opening gambit in explaining how and why we connect race and resistance as we do, we must, to borrow loosely from William James, consider some of the more tender-minded and popular ways of dealing with questions of race, victimhood, and suffering, which stem from the sentimental and melodramatic tradition. Although Harriet Beecher Stowe by no means invented this form of racial imagination, in *Uncle Tom's Cabin* she crystallized it as a lasting mode of popular fiction, one that powerfully informed racial representation for more than one hundred years. Today, it serves as the most common underlying logic in novels, plays, movies, and the news for making sense of race and for granting stories of blacks and whites a kind of closure that they rarely possess in actual events.

On one side of American race melodrama, we find the image of the "bad" or angry and vengeful black, a character often depicted in American fantasy as a bloodthirsty criminal or a rapist with an insatiable primal hunger for virginal white flesh. Traditionally, this figure has provided racists with a formula for transforming black degradation into a guilt-relieving tale of white victimization. On the other side of race melodrama, we find the black victim/hero, whose noble and undeserved suffering evokes white compassion and respect. Harriet Beecher Stowe's Uncle Tom provides the most famous example of this type, but he reappears in a wide range of characters, both male and female, actual and fictional. Commonly, Americans gain a great deal of guilt relief through their compassion for such noble figures, but it is not necessary for the "Tom" character type to display nobility in order to inspire sympathy. He only has to suffer.

The appeal of the "Tom" figure inheres in his confirmation of black skin as the very presence of suffering, thus making possible a masochistic identification with his unfortunate condition that reinforces racial compassion to the same degree that it fortifies racial separation. In other words, "Tom" suffers for the sins of his guilty audience, which feels its goodness by tearfully witnessing his grimaces and groans. His status as both insider and extreme outsider makes him a perfect catalyst for the production of sentiment in a rather seductive form. Although his audience might wish for his suffering to end, it still remains complicit with his punishment, even to the point of insistence. As Linda Williams shows in *Playing the Race Card*, the logic of race melodrama reaches its apex in a kind of compassionate violence, as in the motion picture *The Green Mile*, where a black Jesus figure—who miraculously heals almost everyone he encounters by absorbing their pain into his gigantic body—is executed by the very whites who love him the most. Watching these white men carry out his execution with tenderness and care, the audience could follow the hallowed rules of race melodrama by regarding deep love for a pure and virtuous black man as a proper remedy for the guilt of having to kill him unjustly in the name of the state. Nevertheless, one might still hope that at least some of the audience would recognize the great divide of justice and sympathy in this scene and vote with justice. Unfortunately, given the history of popular American thought on the race question, this seems unlikely.

Still, despite its grand contribution to interracial dishonesty, it remains important to recognize the good that the sentimental and melodramatic imagination has wrought. Almost everyone knows of the role *Uncle Tom's Cabin* played in the popularization of antislavery sentiment. Also, over the years, melodrama has proven just as useful for blacks as it has for whites. The dramatization of undeserved black suffering at the hands of evil and ignorant whites or within the clutches of a biased and cruel "system" has provided one of the best weapons in the arsenal of the black freedom movement. This weapon, when skillfully wielded, has combined suffering and resistance, galvanizing blacks and whites into making justified claims against the system. It has also led at times to genuine sympathy between the races and to the passage of laws that have undeniably advanced American democracy.

Among its indirect effects on the advancement of democracy, the sentimental and melodramatic racial imagination has stood behind the most common constructions of the black rebel, who turns the passivity of the "Tom" figure into heroic action and converts the dangerous primitivism of the "anti-Tom" into passionate, principled resistance. Rather than submit to the role of the abject sufferer, many blacks, from Frederick Douglass to the black power protesters of the 1960s, have preferred to imagine themselves along these lines. In this way, they have attempted to undo the terms of both the negrophilic "Tom" and the negrophobic "anti-Tom" tendencies of white American racial discourse. Yet the underlying melodramatic logic remains the same. Seeing the black rebel as a hero requires a certain sympathy with her victimized state, which ratifies her rebellion in proportion to the severity of her victimization. Sometimes this means viewing her as having been removed from a previous state of innocence, perhaps in Africa or in the South, to which she symbolically or literally returns in the act of resistance. At other times it means contemplating her alienation from family or from some other basic category of human belonging. Regardless of the particular source of undeserved suffering, the formula remains the same: as the inversion of Tom, the rebel never fully leaves him behind. He simply transmutes the cry of the sufferer into the shout of righteous protest.

Developed along melodramatic and sentimental lines, the black rebel may stand out for his courage, his sense of justice, or his deft timing in taking direct action, but sincerity is his best calling card. Unlike his sometimes equally rebellious but unprincipled counterpart, the trickster figure, he signifies on the outside exactly what he feels in his heart. This quality touches us when the famous teardrop rolls down Frederick Douglass's cheek in the *Narrative* as he remembers the joyful slave songs that filled the air at the Great House Farm, but it chills when Richard Wright's Bigger Thomas, headed down a Green Mile of his own, utters with equal sincerity, "What I killed for, I *am*!"

On the list of ethical values that modernity has granted special importance, *sincerity* may have the greatest range of application. From the bedroom to the political podium, the honest soul who can show his true feelings makes himself a candidate for praise. "Show me that you really mean it." On the one hand, the lover with a ready response to this request may earn a delicious gift. The black slave, on the other hand, may only gain the reward of survival. For him, the game of sincerity had particularly high stakes because the black-white racial divide assumed a gap so great that the masters always had to wonder if something they could never know went on behind appearances. Of course, they preferred to believe that no distance obtained between the black signifier and signified and found comfort in whatever evidence seemed to support the wish. Bequeathed to later generations, this wish became one of the true stalwarts of the American racial imagination, even to the point of making possible certain acts of white sincerity. One only has to think here of Al Jolson's blackface routine in *The Jazz Singer*, where his character, Jakie Rabinowitz, communicates his love for his mother as he leaves the ghetto and the world of his dead father, the cantor at the Orchard Street synagogue. Now, as a real American, he can love his mother the way a Negro supposedly loves his mammy. One imagines that he could not have signified this kind of deep love through the native gestures of his new white identity—that he could be true to himself and others only by adopting the mask.

Among its many effects, the desire for black sincerity produced in the slave, and in her segregated and otherwise racially circumscribed descendants, a peculiar fascination with the honest soul. We might even speculate that the popular idea of black soulfulness, as a matter of religion, food, and music, has something to do with the black need to claim ownership over this idea. One only has to think for a moment about such masters in the art of avowal as Harriet Jacobs, Smokey Robinson, and Louis Farrakhan to recognize some of the unique ways that African Americans have developed this mode. Given its elaborate presence in African American culture, it hardly surprises that sincerity would provide a strong resource for the black rebel figure both in art and in life. Rather than rooting performance in the fear of paranoid white oppressors, the rebel transforms the act of meaning what one says into a matter of courage and group solidarity—in other words, into something that can work for African Americans as a sign of defiance and freedom.

Given the centrality of sincerity as a racial value for both blacks and whites, it stands to reason that the honest soul—whether as a loyal house servant, a country bumpkin, or an earnest advocate of racial solidarity—would become one of black laughter's favorite targets. The same forces that made black Americans focus with special intensity on the development of sincere modes of expression also inspired a fascination with characters that either could not or would not say anything they meant. Br'er Rabbit, the signifyin' Monkey, and other trickster figures of African American folklore provide a long tradition along these lines. The wonderful speeches in Ralph Ellison's *Invisible Man*, inspired in their own way by the trickster tradition, offer another. In these, humor arises in part out of the protagonist's inability to say anything that he means, mostly out of his desire to look like an honest soul. Caring only about his appearance to the crowd, he cannot begin to master himself. Still, he succeeds in moving his listeners, but only when he loses control, and on a basis that he cannot understand. Rather than disqualifying him from black leadership, this makes him the perfect candidate. Similarly, the speech by Shakespeare Agamemnon Beard, a thinly veiled parody of W.E.B. Du Bois, in George Schuyler's *Black No More* highlights through humorous exaggeration just how self-defeating the act of racial sincerity can become. In his effort to rally a group of black leaders to prevent the sale of a formula that will end the race problem, and their race hustle, by turning black people white, he invokes his own special version of the "old-time religion": reminiscent of the high-toned rhetoric of such works as *Darkwater* and *The Souls of Black Folk*, he assures his listeners that their destiny lies in the stars. He invokes in quick succession "Ethiopia's fate," "the bitter tears of the Goddess of the Nile," "The Great Sphinx," "the lowering clouds over the Congo," and "lightning flashing o'er Togoland," and concludes with an Old Testament flourish: "To your tents, O Israel! The hour is at hand." In the face of such an appeal, even the duplicitous leaders of black America had to acknowledge the imperative of racial resistance, which in this case meant saving the Negro from his desire to escape the race problem by the most efficient technical means ever invented—a magic elixir.

Among its effects, this scene highlights through parody the self-deconstructing tendency of sincerity. The better or more consciously crafted the act is, the more it looks like an act. According to Lionel Trilling's *Sincerity and Authenticity*, the intimate relationship between sincerity and deception slowly contributed to the displacement of sincerity as a dominant social value in the West by the late nineteenth century, although, as the examples above indicate, it continued to hold a solid place on the list of modern virtues. Sincerity received its first recognition as a praiseworthy quality of the individual in the sixteenth and seventeenth centuries, when the European class structure of the Middle Ages started to erode and give way to an expanding social sphere. At this point, Trilling points out, men and women of all stations could cross paths and, if they dared, pretend to a higher social station than they actually occupied. Such fakers threatened social hierarchy in a number of ways, but most crucially by exposing everyone else as a faker. If aristocracy could be effectively imitated, or reduced to mere social performance, what of the claims it made to noble blood? Thus arose the comforting idea of the honest soul, who would presumably never dream of misrepresenting himself. The parallel between this kind of class mobility feared by aristocratic Europeans in the sixteenth and seventeenth centuries and the type of racial passing that we know well in the United States does appear worth noting here, especially given the role of sincerity in both cases as an answer to ruling-class anxieties about the supposed danger of improper contact. Whether or not we regard the class-oriented anxieties of early modern Europeans as "racial" in some connection, it would seem remiss to ignore the role of race, the slave trade, and colonialism in expanding European wealth in the sixteenth and seventeenth centuries, and thus in contributing to the underlying conditions that made sincerity possible. As these conditions threatened established class lines and made the prerogatives of heredity harder to defend, they eventually inspired new race-based ideas of blood and inheritance that remain with us today.

In *Racism: A Short History*, the historian George Fredrickson traces the idea of race back to medieval Christian notions of a heritable curse against the Jews for refusing to follow Christ, but he finds the origin of the modern biological version of this idea in the Enlightenment attempt to erect a naturalistic and rationalistic account of man. The racial classification systems of such early race theorists as Linnaeus, Blumenbach, and Buffon directly expressed the intellectual aspiration of this period to replace medieval superstition and the Great Chain of Being with rationality and scientific knowledge aimed at the expansion of human powers based on the domination of nature. The augmentation of human happiness and the reduction of suffering through scientific technique and the protective efforts of the state stood as major justifications of this new dispensation, which spawned modern-day racism at the same time that it gave birth to the rights of man, equality, universalism, and almost every other value commonly evoked to explain why racism should not exist.

From a philosophical standpoint, the Enlightenment set rational man in one sphere and disenchanted nature in another, making a reconciliation between the two almost impossible to conceive. Of course, human beings had a foot in each camp, and according to some of the most famous Enlightenment thinkers, such as Hume, Jefferson, and Rousseau, the darker humans leaned into the camp of nature and the lighter ones into the camp of civilization. It follows from the hierarchical implications of such a conception that Enlightenment thinkers would tend to split humankind into groups spread across a spectrum from the most civilized to the least, from the most human to the most animal-like, and from the modern present to the primitive past, corresponding to supposedly observable and scientifically verifiable characteristics, and to political facts of the day such as colonialism and slavery, which they tended to explain as just consequences of the hierarchy of knowledge. In the end, this reduced to a new version of a very old idea: might makes right.

For students of race relations, the invention of scientific or color-coded racism stands out as a telling dimension of Enlightenment thought, but we must look to the primary role that this period gave to resistance in order to understand more clearly the racial dispensation that it has handed down to us. Of course, resistance has marked relations between oppressor and oppressed from the beginning of human history. Interpreting the concept broadly, we might even regard it as an indispensable part of what it means to be human, but this would get us closer to modern conceptions of resistance like those of Freud, Nietzsche, and Marx than it would to the conscious motivations of rebellious slaves, serfs, and other oppressed groups in earlier epochs. In contrast to premodern conceptions of opposition, which typically involved ideas of tradition, authority, and the supernatural, the Enlightenment turned resistance into a singular virtue at one with the larger effort to employ power and rationality in transforming nature and society to increase health, wealth, cultural development, and other specifically human productions. Thus transformed, resistance became an indispensable concept for the interpretation of everyday life, from the constitution of the modern subject to the everyday struggles of the average worker.

Even more important for our purposes, the Enlightenment revaluation of resistance inaugurated opposition as the only possible authentic gesture of the oppressed, and as the supreme litmus test of their humanity. By tying the value of freedom to the core meaning of rationality and by making this a central criterion of humanity, the thinkers of the Enlightenment invented a wholly new way to link violence from below to the possibility of a better and more harmonious human existence, a line of thinking that played out both gloriously and tragically in the creative destruction of the French, Haitian, and American revolutions. To this source we also owe the common tendency to associate the assertion of black humanity with physical or cultural resistance to slavery and other forms of racist oppression. Scholars like Herbert Aptheker, who carried out the first assiduous search for evidence of rebellion among African American slaves, and many others who continue to find consistent opposition to racist hegemony in African American literature, speech, modes of self-fashioning, or family structure remain heavily invested in this equation between revolutionary violence and historical progress.

Of the many ideas arising from the Enlightenment transformation of resistance, none has had a greater impact on the subsequent course of human events than the concept of *revolution*. As Hannah Arendt has pointed out at length in *On Revolution*, the notion of a violent and sudden upheaval of human agency transforming the course of history came about with the invention of history itself, which arose in connection with the new emphasis on change within a contingent universe. Indeed, the very shaping of agency as a major goal of modem individual and collective life bears a strong relationship to the ultimately violent idea of employing power to alter the flow of events. The Haitian Revolution comes immediately to mind in this connection, as well as the instances of revolutionary rhetoric among African American Marxists and Nationalists throughout the twentieth century. We might also recognize the idea of sudden transformation through violence in Frederick Douglass's epic wrestling match with the slave driver Covey in the *Narrative*, where he claims to have escaped slavery spiritually long before he broke away physically.

Yet a full understanding of Douglass's meaning in this passage requires more than the secular context of Enlightenment thought. The emphasis on immediate conversion evokes images of sudden transformation in the vein of Paul on the road to Damascus. The wrestling match with Covey conjures associations with the Old Testament story of Jacob, who demanded and received a blessing from the angel of God after wrestling him to a stalemate for an entire night. After this experience, Jacob claimed proudly to have looked God in the face and survived. One supposes that Frederick Douglass wanted to claim the same of the Devil. Pushing the comparison between Jacob and Douglass a bit further, it also seems important that the patriarch's blessing involved a name change (to Israel) that conferred on him the leadership of a nation—surely an optimistic thought for an escaped African American slave. Yet Old Testament analogies of this sort, especially those involving the Jewish exodus from Egypt, convinced many African American slaves that God held them in His special favor. By comparing their lowly condition with that of Jewish slaves in the Bible, they could envision a glorious future of inevitable freedom. Although we should avoid the trap of reducing African American religion to resistance, it remains important to recognize its central role in resistant thinking from the earliest days of slave Christianity, to Nat Turner, to the slave narratives, to the development of the black freedom movement in the nineteenth and twentieth centuries.

As we recognize the important role of religion in the history of African American resistance, we might also note that to a more secular tradition of resistant thought and practice, which includes most versions of Marxism and a large bandwidth of liberalism, such faith-based conceptions of opposition count for little or nothing. By speaking a language of God, miracles, revelation, and resurrection, they place the ultimate fate of the world outside the scope of human powers and beyond the reach of politics—a fatal flaw according to those who seek secular solutions to social problems. Sometimes this conviction has inspired downright vitriolic claims: for example, that religion reduces to superstition or to a retrograde unwillingness to face the world that men and women must control in order to live better lives. Even when this secular tradition recognizes that religion plays a role in the advancement of human freedom, it rarely includes faith on the list of ultimate solutions. At best, it casts religion as a way station to freedom, but it does not do even this very often.

Although the tendency to begrudge religion has many sources, none stands out more than the heavy weight that secular Western thought places on the idea of self-constituting subjects and groups—a thought that flows directly from the fundamental dependence of ideas like free government, civil society, and the market on a ground-level conception of human autonomy that depends on nothing outside of itself. In some ways, this idea takes us directly to the second member of Lionel Trilling's famous pair, the idea of *authenticity*. As opposed to the sincere individual, who looks outward to society for confirmation of his performance, the authentic self remains firmly rooted in his or her sentiment of being, or the feelings arising from the most fundamental presocial source of existence. In this connection we might say that the authentic self simply "is": rather than being true to others, she is true to herself. Where sincerity faces the crowd, authenticity shirks confirmation. In contrast to sincerity's equation of surface and depth, authenticity sometimes dons a mask to tell its truth—all the better to reflect the ultimately invisible origins of its message.

Nevertheless, like sincerity, authenticity can also fall prey to a kind of mechanical or stale social performance. This appears all the more likely when large numbers of people within a society look to each other for ways to achieve it. If sincerity fails in its unwillingness to acknowledge how deeply it depends on acting, authenticity errs in denying its need for acknowledgment. In the end it is probably impossible simply to "be" while depending all along on others to recognize that one does not care about recognition. Thus, authenticity may better represent the bind of modern selfhood than its salvation. Perhaps this explains why so many of us in pursuit of this high value fall prey instead to confusion, paranoia, rage, narcissism, and cruelty.

The idea of authenticity received early crystallization in the philosophy of Jean-Jacques Rousseau, whose outlook reflects well its promise, its perils, and the connection of both to resistance against established authority. Rousseau inverted the direction of social contract theory put forward by Hobbes, Locke, and Hume—and the preference for civilized sophistication among his Enlightenment contemporaries—by regarding the state of society as inherently corrupt and the state of nature as a preferred condition where human beings live in virtuous harmony with creation. Describing the development of society through various stages, he criticizes the development of tools, language, medicine, property, and modes of human association for their corrupting effect on man's original robust constitution, savage independence, self-love, and natural compassion for the suffering of beings like himself. The development of science and the arts only made matters worse by adding sugarcoating and lies, what we today would call *ideology*, to the corrosive force of society. In the end, Rousseau's suspicious picture of civilized life provided excellent reasons for every human being to regard every other as a danger to his most fundamental sense of integrity. An idea of total resistance seems to apply here, where individuals must defend their truest and most natural selves against every aspect of the world around them, including their own culture and education.

Yet Rousseau feared that the best efforts of the lone individual would always yield to the mammoth virtue-destroying force of society. Thus, he found hope in a highly regimented version of collective will, which he expected the individual to follow without question. Although we might trace some ideas of democratic majority rule to this source, its clearest legacy resides in totalitarianism and fascism. Perhaps this points up best the strong relationship between Rousseau's ideas of authenticity and paranoia; yet we must not go too far in making such a link. Rousseau's unprecedented account of inequality stands as a genuinely liberating force in modern thought without which it would be hard to imagine the great range of Western social movements from Marxism to liberal reform.

Ideas of authenticity and virtue receive a rich expression in Rousseau's philosophy that helps us to understand the enduring appeal of racial resistance for African Americans as a way of being true to something fundamental and virtuous against the efforts of a corrupt, or racist, society that seeks to undermine or distort contact with an important source of meaning. We might also see in the suspicious attitude toward social arrangements, especially when the suspicion involves the defense of an immediate and natural ideal of blackness, a direct link to the matrix of concepts in Rousseau. In this connection, the notion of "keeping it real" might take on a philosophical aura. If it is really true, as some sociologists of education have said, that black boys and girls sometimes associate the attainment of education with the discreditable desire to be white, we may say that they have, at least implicitly, learned a little Rousseau, even if their early quest to be true to themselves might frustrate efforts to teach them much else. But we do not have to pick on children to find our best examples, because authenticity has had long career in African American thought—in part because it provides an ethical perch for the individual outside of the social arena, where racial problems and definitions arise. It figures prominently, although very differently, in the work of Hurston, Ellison, Schuyler, and Baldwin, as it does in most of the writing classifiable under the broad label of literary modernism. In the work of these writers, the quest for authenticity tends to set the black individual as much against the conventions of the black community, itself corrupted in various ways by its accommodation to racism, as it does against the larger oppressive society. Such complex dynamics of resistance and authenticity can make these authors hard to read as resisters in any linear sense, although some critics have managed to do just this.

Using the philosophy of Rousseau as a lens, we tend to focus more on the individualist strains of African American authenticity than on its collective aspects, which figure heavily in nationalism, in multiculturalism, and in movements aiming at the discovery, enhancement, and projection of subjective states of black consciousness such as the Harlem Renaissance and the Black Arts Movement. Here the nineteenth-century development of expressivist thought comes into play. Fundamentally, the expressivist strain complicates the idea of a universal humanity by taking an anthropological approach to the problem of human essence. Instead of employing a unitary measure of humanness, such as rationality, it regards the common values, folkways, and languages of large cultural groups as equally valuable expressions of a multiform humanity. We might detect in this idea certain echoes of Rousseau's concept of a collective will, but this time shorn of its more sinister implications and enhanced with a more inclusive concept of virtue. Nevertheless, we might also recognize something sinister in how easily this apparently pluralistic account of human virtue lends itself to race thinking on the grand historical scale, with particular cultural groups regarded as races and nations living out ideas of collective destiny based on the possession of traits, qualities, and common forms of language that represent their most authentic way of being.

Because it gives the possession of group characteristics such high-level significance, expressivism can sometimes inspire an almost religious attitude concerning their protection and preservation. Although this outlook defends from instrumentalist reduction such flexible and contingent quantities as common language and beliefs, it tends to make them almost wholly self-justifying simply because groups of people share them. Individuals seeking to cast themselves in authentic terms may therefore find a powerful anchor in ideas of group feeling or collective spirit, especially when they regard these group orientations as somehow endangered by outside forces such as capitalism, racism, or imperialism. We might imagine that the current penchant for asserting group identity within an ethnic, religious, or racial group against a monochromatic, normalizing—and therefore threatening and powerful—mainstream participates in this thought. Ironically, so do the most overt assertions of "white" identity, which usually take attacks on the mainstream by dissenters as the defining backdrop for the assertion of group feeling.

African American thought abounds in different versions of expressivism, almost all of which maintain a strong association with ideas of resistance. In fact, we might spend the rest of the day reciting them, because most major works in the African American tradition travel down this broad boulevard of Western thought to reach their various destinations. Du Bois evokes expressivism in *The Souls of Black Folk* when he optimistically counts African Americans as the latest addition to a list of world historical peoples that includes the Teuton and the Mongolian. Marcus Garvey did the same when he exclaimed, "Up you mighty race!" in urging blacks around the world to rise and seize their destiny. Helene Johnson in "Sonnet to a Negro in Harlem" taps into the same vein of thought when she praises a "disdainful" yet "magnificent" Harlemite for his rejection of the tired norms of the American mainstream. In a somewhat different register, James Weldon Johnson's protagonist in *Autobiography of an Ex-Colored Man* invokes black authenticity when he fears that in abandoning his race he has sold his soul "for a mess of pottage." So does Malcolm X when he abandons the "processed" hair of the street hustler, rejects the white man's religion, and joins the Nation of Islam. On the popular front, Afros, dashikis, soul food, black power, black beauty, and black love all represent versions of group-oriented authenticity in one way or another. Even current ideas of a new black aesthetic or a postsoul culture, which resist romantic ideas of authenticity and pat conceptions of black rebellion, still tap into ideas of being true to oneself and to one's group as they attempt to maintain the sharp edge of black cultural opposition and multicultural complexity.

Events in the presidential race of 2008 highlight the continuing centrality of authenticity for African Americans and the ways that this category overlaps with the idea of resistance. When he began his run for the presidency, Barack Obama might have seemed a shoo-in for garnering a large portion of the African American vote, just as Al Sharpton and Jesse Jackson had before him. Nevertheless, many African Americans withheld support from him because they questioned his blackness, and with this his credentials as a resister. Still others wondered whether white Americans would vote for a black candidate, even one so carefully distanced from black resistance as Obama. Thus, somewhere between judging Obama too black and not black enough, many African Americans decided that the smart money ought to go on Hillary Clinton, whose husband, Bill, had built his presidency on a stealthy combination of handpicked Republican economic policies, traditional liberalism, and a capacity to project sympathy in the classic mode of the sincere man of the people. Blacks provided the main litmus test for Clinton's ability to feel the pain of the suffering electorate, and he performed his role with such skill that the novelist Toni Morrison, half-seriously taking his penchant for marital infidelity and junk food as evidence, named him our first black president. As Bill Clinton's long-suffering partner, Hillary benefited vicariously from this association. Also, as a powerful advocate for blacks in her own right, she held strong appeal for many black voters, notwithstanding the tantalizing possibility represented by Obama: that the second black president of the United States might actually be black.

Having based his candidacy on the idea of unifying the nation, largely due to his crazy-quilt multiracial background,

Obama had, according to a few observers, signed a pact with the American people to represent racial progress while mentioning race hardly at all. Yet, when it began to look like Obama could actually win, blacks began supporting him in large numbers, making the racial implications of his run for the presidency hard to ignore. More than any other single fact, this signaled to the Democratic electorate that the same multiracial background that marked Obama's ability to bring the country together could just as easily represent forces that threatened to tear it apart. Questions that seemed safely buried during the early days of his candidacy began to surface like the living dead: Is Obama a Muslim? Is he anti-Semitic? Is he antipatriotic? Is he an angry black man in disguise? Suddenly, the candidate that some blacks had suspected as a veritable white man in blackface had to answer for his association with such avatars of blackness and resistance as Louis Farrakhan and Jeremiah Wright. The controversy surrounding Wright, Obama's former pastor, has proven particularly difficult for the senator, due in large part to the incessant playing of short video clips on the internet and in the media of the pastor declaring "God damn America!" and proclaiming the 9/11 terrorists attacks "the chickens coming home to roost" in a style reminiscent of the comment that made Elijah Muhammad silence Malcolm X after the Kennedy assassination in November 1963.

Wright's bold oppositional statements played the key role in placing Obama, the shining star of post–civil rights racial advancement, in the seemingly untenable position of calming racially motivated fears that he might harbor unpatriotic black racist feelings. In other words, as the black trickster and bluesman Jim Trueblood from Ralph Ellison's *Invisible Man* might say, the bind of black identity had made it necessary for the senator to "move without movin'." And in his deeply textured, thoughtful, and perhaps historic address in

March 2008 on American race relations, Obama tried to do just this. Reminding everyone of his biracial background, which made him neither white nor black, yet both, he sought to split the difference on Jeremiah Wright by denouncing the pastor's offending statements while embracing the man. In a similar gesture, he declared his undying love for his white grandmother, whose racism sometimes made him cringe, as he sympathized with the misdirected but understandable racial fears of the white working class. Having employed his double agent racial identity to peer across the black and white sides of the racial divide, Obama brought the subtleties of the intimate sphere to bear on the simpleminded sound-bite culture of American public discourse in a fashion that would have pleased the protean storyteller Jim Trueblood very much. Resisting the time-honored binary logic of black and white, evident in the continuing force of the distinctively American one-drop racial standard that marked him as black despite his white mother, he offered himself as the symbol, the embodied beginning, of a complex conversation on race that holds the potential for perfecting the nation through loving acceptance of its imperfections.

At this point in the emerging story of Obama's historic run for the presidency (at the time of this writing), it appears that this formula may well have done the trick. Obama may have slipped the yoke of blackness by making himself the focus of a racial discussion that America has managed to avoid for three hundred years. Yet his presidential hopes probably hinge on deferring this discussion for at least one year more. No one hoping to curry favor with voters could possibly place his hopes on the guilt-laced, fear-ridden insanity of full interracial disclosure. Throughout history messengers have been punished severely for delivering much more benign truths. Can Obama both inspire and defer a conversation on race at the same time? He moved without movin' once, and he will probably have to do so a few more times before the long election season comes to an end.

Such partial observations of an unfinished election may not help us to understand the most important motivations of American voters, but they do point up an important matter in race politics: essentially negative motivations and identifications play a central role. The affirmation of the group almost always comes with an implicit or explicit "no" aimed at some "other," or at a member of the group who has in one way or another gone over to the enemy. In many ways, this follows the general norm of group construction, whether of the ethnic, class-based, or gender-oriented variety, which always involves the fabrication of boundaries around comparisons with what the group is not, or what it should resist. Because basic claims to humanity and justice stand at the core of the race question, boundary construction around issues of black and white has always involved particularly high stakes and strong emotions. Naming what the group is not and trying to avoid whatever discreditable associations make the list go hand in hand with a necessary backdrop of suspicion, especially in contexts like the current one where social dynamism, mobility, and fragmentation threaten the maintenance of boundaries.

We might notice a perennial irony within the terms of such an observation: the association of true blackness with fighting for freedom has always emphasized the breaking of boundaries around race; yet the maintenance of the group, as well as the ability to fight, requires their construction. A necessary tension around what it means to remain true to one's people has always accompanied this bind. Perhaps we owe to it some of the age-old observations about envy, or the "crabs in the barrel" feeling among blacks. Today, fashionable in-group lingo refers to the phenomenon as "player hating," but the basic issue remains the same: Did a member of the group achieve success legitimately or by betraying the group in some way? Should another member of the group question his success, or does this always count as "sour grapes" or as disdain for black achievement? Of course, disdain can work in many directions when such concerns come into play. Those who regard themselves as having "made it" may dislike or feel embarrassed by members of the group who represent powerlessness or the characteristics associated with it. Alternatively, those remaining below may regard marks of achievement as the sign of the traitor. Tensions of this sort are well captured by a joke that I came across in preparing my study on the journalist George Schuyler. A monkey standing in the road begging receives a dime from a white traveler. Before he can get out of the way, a black man speeding down the road runs him over. When the wagon stops, the monkey thinks to himself, "This brother isn't too bad. He's coming back to help *me*." The black man stoops over the monkey. Seeing the dime still clutched in the monkey's paw, he snatches it away and drives off. Sadly shaking his head, the monkey responds, "Our race just won't *do*."

Few writers have ignored the role of such venomous emotions as anger, rage, envy, self-hatred, spite, contempt, and pity in American race relations. Yet, only a few have granted these feelings the foundational place they deserve in the historical construction of black and white. Again, in keeping with my basic theme, I would suggest that such emotions derive as much from the larger circumstance of capitalist modernity, where the possibility of rising or falling in status marks every social station, as they do from the historical particulars of American and African American life. In the book *Ressentiment*, the German philosopher Max Scheler regards negative and venomous emotions as built-in features of modern competitive societies, which emphasize formal rules of equality quite often in the face of large disparities in wealth and status. Developing the idea of ressentiment from the philosophical application of its inventor, Friedrich Nietzsche, into a tool of modern social analysis, Scheler claims that unlike the highly structured class societies of the Middle Ages, in modem society each person can look at the possessions of others and, at least in principle, regard them as potentially her own. Nevertheless, she may feel limited by personal weakness or external circumstance from gaining the desired objects or the characteristics necessary for attaining them. In response, she may convince herself, as in Aesop's story of the fox and the sour grapes, that the desired object itself has no value—that the particular grapes that she cannot reach are not sweet. Alternately, she may convince herself that sweetness is bad or that those who have access to it are hurting themselves and others. Even more abstractly, she may congratulate herself for refusing the seduction of sweets or devote herself to saving people afflicted by their unfortunate addiction to them. We could continue into infinity with this progression, because the self-contradictory tangle of ressentiment develops toward ever higher levels of abstraction, each one more remote from the desired object than the last.

Although it involves strong feelings of hatred and envy, ressentiment almost never involves direct action against the source of bad feeling. In fact, it tends to block true power-seeking behavior. Most characteristically, ressentiment manifests itself in false feelings of benevolence or in the denial of power, as in Nietzsche's treatment in *Genealogy of Morals* of the priests who laud meekness and peace not for their intrinsic merit, but for their usefulness in negating the worldview of the physically superior warriors who defeated them. Yet most exemplars of ressentiment play the game of power much less successfully than Nietzsche's priests. Quite often, the persons who feel ressentiment seek out the company of the individual or group that they despise, sometimes even to the point of seeming obsequiousness. The man or woman of ressentiment may even court abuse in order to confirm feelings of degradation and righteousness. Nevertheless, he or she may still manage to feel sorry for the abusers from some lofty humanitarian standpoint, or alternately in highly abstract terms hate their very existence or the characteristics of their group. The possibilities for self-contradiction never end, for the person of ressentiment holds the negation of the despised other above all else, even to the point of comical self-deception. We might think here of Dostoyevsky's Underground Man, whose concern with defending his honor leads him constantly into degrading situations that he paradoxically relishes for confirming his sense of genius and distinction. We might also think of Ellison's *Invisible Man*, whose problems concerning race, resistance, and identity have the same basic source, a sense of distinction rooted in a seething, self-directed violence.

The arsonist who burns your house down because your presence in the neighborhood makes him feel diminished definitely suffers from ressentiment, but if he does the evil deed because he likes the sight of fire, he has other problems. Likewise, the slave who hates the master for enslaving him stands on solid ground if he really does hate slavery in general, but the one who despises the master for making him feel small, or who desires the master's power despite feeling too weak to get it, has probably fallen into the self-contradictory tangle of ressentiment. Even when men and women of ressentiment evoke principle, their real concerns reduce to the battle for honor, distinction, and the mixed feelings that come with it. Sometimes, as in the case of the old maid who preaches sexual abstinence to the young, the presence of ressentiment may prove simple to detect, but usually this malady dons a more effective disguise, as in the current case of white American color blindness, which employs a benign mask of racial fairness and formal equality to silence resentfully the discussion of continuing racial inequalities. Still, this should not stop us from entertaining a few choice speculations concerning the occasions where the effect of ressentiment on the American racial scene appears most evident.

As a general matter, the connection between race consciousness and ressentiment is easier to recognize in the case of African Americans than in the case of whites. We can all see why African Americans who have never possessed the means to overturn white power would respond to it with a mixture of desire and disdain. The white side of the picture is a bit more complicated, though. If Scheler is right, then the United States must have always been a hotbed of ressentiment in part because of the emphasis its culture has placed on an ideology of unfettered individual achievement. Of course, those who look to rise may also fall, and the progressive culture of the United States has never made much provision for failure, even though the vast majority must finish second or below in any competition. As Tocqueville points out at length in *Democracy in America*, the democratic political culture of the United States inclines individuals to make envious comparisons and to engage in a narcissism of small differences. Caught between the oblivion of falling and the difficulty of rising to sufficient heights, many white Americans have always found comfort in the idea of race, a social concept that places them in a natural aristocracy forever above another group that possesses every characteristic associated with failure. In other words, by allowing whites to project the ugly emotions that accompany the unlimited pursuit of happiness onto a despised other, race has played a key role in guaranteeing the American way of life.

It follows directly from the basic characteristics of ressentiment that white Americans would alternately despise, pity, and love black Americans, even to the point of imitation.

And as whites seek through real and symbolic contact with blacks to recuperate feelings of lost naturalness and virtue—the inevitable fallout of rising toward the Dream—it also follows that they would make an abstraction of the supposedly hideous black essence. Perhaps this explains to some degree why one needs to look no further than the stereotypes of black Americans to locate the deepest and most time-honored American desires: sexual prowess, natural physical ability, immediate emotional satisfaction, transgression of every acceptable social code, and deep, childlike religiosity. These qualities begin a list that might well become many pages of characteristics that whites have projected onto blacks, whom they alternately embrace and reject. In some ways this observation brings us back to Jakie Rabinowitz, the protagonist of *The Jazz Singer*, who could only express his truest and most natural feelings of love toward his mother from behind the minstrel mask, a symbol synonymous with degradation but also with a certain freedom of expression; with falsehood but also with a deeply human truth; and with death but also with the countervailing promise of an all-too-American second chance.

Bringing these observations to a more current conjuncture, it appears that ressentiment plays an even greater role in the atmosphere of the post–civil rights era than it did in the past. Greater acceptance of the principle of racial equality has occurred in the face of an ever-increasing gap in wealth that not only victimizes blacks disproportionately but causes a great fear of falling among all but the richest Americans. At the same time, the black middle class has made an unprecedented rise, even in the face of persistent racial barriers, mostly as a result of affirmative action policies that many whites regard as unfair. Yet, the collective acceptance of racial equality as an important principle makes racialized fears and anxieties almost impossible to express directly.

Instead, as we learn from the research of Lawrence Bobo and others, they get deflected in myriad directions. Ressentiment also appears to have an effect on the other side of the racial divide, where it bears strong affinities with the largely symbolic strategies pursued by black leaders and by the black middle class in general. From the reparations movement to the accusations against Bill Clinton during the primary campaign for making allegedly racist comments on Barack Obama's candidacy, mainstream black political leadership appears to have taken up the strategy of Nietzsche's priests: rather than assaulting the stronger enemy directly, they have decided to make him disdain his own power. Quite often, this technique involves the deployment of high-order, self-justifying victimology aimed at convincing him of his racism, and at propping up the confidence of his accusers. Perhaps this strategy would work if the enemy really was like Nietzsche's warriors, but the slippery post–civil rights form of white racism rarely expresses itself in a full-throated fashion. In fact, many supposedly powerful whites already think of themselves as real or potential victims of one sort or another. One only needs to reflect for a moment on the war in Iraq, hysterics over terrorism, or the gigantic background of private fear and paranoia now possessing the country, to become downright paranoid about the prospect of becoming the victim of some other victim's gesture of self-defense.

Freedom, Equality, Race

Our current era of race relations in America maintains racial distinctions largely through the expectation that they will soon disappear. This stands in contrast with previous periods, in which such categories as black and white counted as durable facts of descent and destiny. One side of the current race debate plays up the disappearance of racial distinctions, sometimes by exaggerating the virtues of color blindness. The other side guards against the diminishment of such distinctions, at times going so far as to equate current racial problems with the dark and distant past of slavery and Jim Crow. For the first camp—what we might call a "party of hope"—current racial realities signal the promise of a raceless future where skin color may have no more societal import than does eye color. The second—a "party of memory"—aims for a similar goal, but it generally casts its ultimate purpose in more pluralistic terms. This party finds the waning of timeworn forms of racial identity, along with the deeply etched barriers that gave rise to them, threatening to the very political movements that might bring about lasting positive change. Ironically, the party of memory finds what the party of hope would call racial progress somewhat dangerous to ultimate racial justice. No less curious is the party of hope's prevailing expectation that after more than two hundred years of constant racial strife, black and white identity in the United States will simply fade away.

In some ways, the expectation that race will disappear seems particular to our era of race relations; but in other ways, the thought goes back quite far. Most Americans have always regarded the abiding values of our country as universal, and therefore raceless. Because they think of such principles as equality and freedom in this way, they believe that eventually, in an essentially good and fair country such as ours, these high ideals will prevail over the more parochial values that keep us apart. Historically, this progressive mind-set has come with many good intentions on the race question but much less follow-up. For this and other reasons it has long been an object of attack for scholars of the African American experience. Those who believe that racial problems will go away on their own tend not to act directly to solve them, or they put forth half-stepping measures that address some issues but invent, reinvent, or exacerbate others. Over time, this tendency has contributed mightily to the cloud of betrayal that hangs constantly, and sometimes ominously, over the American racial discourse. At its worst, the seemingly benign idea of progress, which many still regard as the soul of the American Dream, can serve as a mask for crass class interest, or can allow racists to "blame the victim" and thus to deny the cruel meaning of their antidemocratic views. Yet these consequences of progress do not contradict the meaning of such foundational values as freedom and equality so much as they manifest their inner logic.

It is worth remembering the uncomfortable and often repeated fact that our most cherished American principles have as one of their most important sources the minds of slave masters and slave traders. Discerning observers of the American experience, such as the historian Edmund Morgan, have demonstrated a necessary relationship between the freedom cries of slave masters and their status as absolute rulers of stateless men and women who were regarded primarily as property, and as human beings in a much less formal register. In *American Slavery, American Freedom* (1975), Morgan argues that ruling-class Southerners at the time of the American Revolution—Patrick Henry, for example—tended to associate all subordination with the wretched condition of their slaves.[1] They employed this analogy in their idealistic insistence on freedom from the British. Henry's famous eruption on the floor of the Continental Congress, "Give me liberty or give me death," marked him as a radical republican, one ready to pay the highest price for independence. Nevertheless, the reverberant utterance of this slave-holding Virginian (and others like him) bequeathed a cruel legacy to generations of Americans. Unlike free white men, Henry's slaves lived under the very condition that would presumably have driven their freedom-loving master to kill and to die. Henry's formulation, oddly, justified the degradation of African Americans by the very condition that the degradation caused; in no small measure, it associated blackness with shame. Though they lived to guarantee the freedom of supposedly independent men and yearned for freedom in their own terms despite their abasement, African Americans suffered for how starkly they symbolized what white men both feared and despised.

Many writers have observed that the Enlightenment, through its emphasis on human powers, gave freedom its modern meaning; but it also codified the modern idea of race as one way to distinguish those worthy of liberty from the irrational, uncivilized, and superstitious "others" who supposedly lived in a perpetual past. In other words, this period handed down most of the reasons to believe in race along with the justifications for despising and resisting it. As the Enlightenment gave life to the modern concept of race, it created the conditions that force us to explain and theorize this category incessantly. In the hands of early race theorists such as Linnaeus, Blumenbach, and de Buffon, seemingly objective biological categories like skin color and skull size served as impartial measures that positioned man as a subject of his own scientific inquiry and thus as an object of new forms of power/knowledge that enabled the shaping and control of populations. Thus, human freedom in this era, and thereafter, depended crucially on a thoroughgoing form of subjection that created its own human hierarchies, which in some ways reinscribed ancient ideas of descent and inheritance but now with a new and highly influential scientific imprimatur. As the modern concept of freedom carried with it the inclusive language of universalism, it also privileged certain human qualities: rationality, possession of nature or property, power, resistance, and autonomy, to name a few. Instead of membership in humanity as it is, freedom signified communion with humanity as it *ought to be*. Those who failed to qualify for this imagined ideal often faced terrible consequences, as the long history of slavery, imperialism, sexism, and class oppression demonstrates amply.

From their inception, the concepts of freedom and race have reinforced each other in the making of modernity; they continue to do so today, though the concept of race has shifted in its definitional grounding, from nature to culture. Despite the fact that some of the old biological valences remain active, the post–civil rights concept of race relies mainly on values, modes of signifying, and behavior. Rather than membership in a biological group, "whiteness" represents a cultural norm that nonwhites may receive rewards for adopting—though acquiring the necessary cultural capital to do so can prove almost impossible for many. Here, as the social theorist Étienne Balibar points out, the work of exclusion occurs through the regulation of inclusion rather than forming an absolute line of demarcation between the races.[2] Those able to conform to the normalizing logic of post–civil rights "whiteness" live freer lives than those who cannot, as the dismal statistics showing racial disparities in wealth, health, education, and criminal justice reveal so evidently. Under this regime, the work of racial exclusion can occur quite efficiently but without overt racism. In contrast with the frontal assault of the pre–civil rights racial regime, which occurred more or less in the open, the new dispensation conducts most of its oppressive labor behind a smokescreen of elaborate racial etiquette and discursive deflection that communicates racial fear and aversion across an ever wider range of signification.

In its more recent cultural guise, race continues to play a strategic role on the exclusionary side of modern freedom; for the excluded, however, racial identity still has deep attractions, partly because the sheer existence of barriers to full social advancement provides a backdrop against which group solidarity might be perceived in moral terms: as part of a long and righteous struggle for freedom. This idea is well established among African Americans, who, out of the necessity of historic struggle, have formed an alternately heroic, sacrificial, and sometimes melodramatic sense of group belonging laden with collective memories of struggle on the wrong side of the American color line. These struggles have served not only as ways of acquiring freedom, but also as a means of performing it culturally and politically across a great range that encompasses modes of self-fashioning, artistic styles, and direct forms of political resistance and protest. This tradition of performing freedom has helped raise African American identity above the level of mere external imposition as it has created a point of identification for those outside the group to symbolize their own freedom struggles.

As a dominant value in American life, freedom has always stood beside and competed with the idea of equality. Nowhere has the complex relationship between these two bedrock concepts had greater impact than in the history of race relations, and rarely has their mutual opposition and entanglement received more trenchant treatment than in the work of the nineteenth-century French aristocrat and social theorist Alexis de Tocqueville. In his classic *Democracy in America* (1840), he observed that in a country where all men are created equal, those not recognized as equals may not be regarded as men. Tocqueville's eminently logical formula sets out in elegant form the intimate connection between a high universal ideal and a foundational violence that it maintains through masking. Following Tocqueville's calculation, hierarchies of descent grow naturally from the inner tensions of democratic values, not out of a failure to attend to them. Americans constantly reinvent racial distinctions and invidious race theories in part to resolve the quandary of their national condition, which entails basic equality on one side and a battle for individual distinction or status on the other.

Basing his observations on an extensive tour of the United States during the 1830s, Tocqueville regarded American society as a test case for the prospects of a new and inexorable world-historical process in which equality, individualism, and democracy would increasingly displace privilege based on birth and permanent class structures. He contemplated America at an early stage of its development with the chaos and despotism of postrevolutionary France, and the slipping grip of his own class, well in view. Though he recognized the positive potential of democracy, he remained equally cognizant of its constitutional flaws: its tendencies toward conformity, dictatorship of the people, corruption, greed, envy, moralism, intellectual shallowness, voluntary isolation of the individual from collective life, and many other weaknesses both large and small. For Tocqueville, American society in the 1830s represented a wonderful opportunity to observe whether such defective tendencies would prevail because it offered a perfect photo-negative of the European social picture: a place where sheer newness put immigrants and near-immigrants, strangers to the land with no permanent barrier between them, in a society where they might arrange life according to their tastes, talents, and desires. Many of the saving graces and sustaining patterns that Tocqueville recognized in American democracy—its local associations and communal public life, its ascetic faith in the value of work, its dynamic and expansive world-altering will—stand endangered in our own age; thus, we may still wonder about the ultimate survivability of our way of life. Or, in light of American race relations from slavery to the present, we might wonder whether Tocqueville understood entirely the full array of forces that have made American democracy cohere. In the end, the stability of our democracy may depend as much on the maintenance of racial inequality, vouchsafed by the anxieties of equality, as it does on the values and structures that Tocqueville so famously cited.

Without "blackness," or some such negative or countervailing category, "whiteness" would not have achieved its stability as the primary mode of identification in America. And without the stabilizing effect of "blackness," one of the main justifications for the average white person to count himself a member of the same group as the richest would not exist. As several important scholars of whiteness studies, such as David Roediger, Noel Ignatiev, and Matthew Frye Jacobson, have shown, this formula has provided one of the greatest bulwarks against the formation of entrenched class identity, even as Americans of all colors and persuasions strive to climb the class ladder partly by blending in.[3] Whiteness, with all its confused connotations of universality and particularity, of destiny and sheer emptiness, still prevails as a reason for some of the poorest Americans to tolerate their condition, even as demographers anticipate the day, not more than a few decades from now, when the American majority will, in numbers, take on a darker hue.

In his famous section "On the Three Races That Currently Inhabit America," Tocqueville contributed a foundational pillar to a long tradition of social analysis that would regard the problem of black and white as an aberration rather than a constitutive feature of American social and political life. Though he analyzes the slave South in detail, he treats it as the opposite of the industrial North, which for him represented the future of American democracy because of its burgeoning productivity, its culture of equality, and the competitive anxiety of its citizens. In the South, he surmised, the existence of slavery retarded development. Rather than productive, the South was lazy; instead of progressive, it remained mired in the past. Lacking ingenuity, it depended on a narrow range of cash crops; lacking equality, it suffered from the absence of inner drive in its rank-and-file citizens, who depended on relatively unproductive slaves to do most of the work. None of these characteristics augured well for the survival of the South. Underdeveloped by its own economic and cultural commitments, faced with an expansive and dynamic sectional competitor, and threatened by the natural increase of its slave population, it faced an imminent crisis. In time, Tocqueville imagined, the South would lose its grip on its slaves, in part because these unfree people, as members of a society that prized equality, would never accept their unequal station, and thus could never embrace the spirit of European peasantry. Yet, he thought, whites would never admit blacks as equals. A racist himself, Tocqueville believed that whites everywhere in the United States would understandably continue to discriminate against an inferior people, and that blacks stood little chance beyond establishing their own state by conducting a war against indolent Southern whites. Given their numbers, and what he regarded as the decrepit moral state of their white enemies, he liked their chances in such a conflict.[4]

Tocqueville's analysis of race in "On the Three Races That Currently Inhabit America" commands current interest much more for its connection to his larger theory than for its historical accuracy. Much of what he anticipated simply did not happen. Moreover, few current historians of American slavery would take up his dichotomous view of North and South, his dim account of slavery's profitability, his unitary view of the slave system, or his somewhat mechanical rendering of the effects of the peculiar institution on the hearts, minds, and motivations of slaves and slaveholders. Nevertheless, Tocqueville's theoretical terms in *Democracy in America* do provide a good foundation for understanding how the value of equality helped reinforce the perennial American obsession with racial distinction.

Tocqueville believed that white Americans, beyond their motivations rooted in racism, would find black Americans hard to accept because of the radically unequal station from which they started. Locked in an absorbing competition with their peers and exceedingly nervous about the prospects of rising and falling in the game of distinction, white Americans would always feel compromised by their association with a degraded and inferior people; their anxiety derived in part from how perfectly the condition of congenital inferiority and social invisibility reflected their own worst fears. The promise of American life, rooted in the idea that no permanent social barrier stands between even the lowest white man and the very richest, comes with the devastating prospect of freefall: those who can rise infinitely can also fall into uncharted territory of vulnerability, invisibility, and loss. Cut off from strong claims to a primordial past and staked on the prospect of ever better days to come, white Americans needed to invent the nigger—the nameless, faceless incompetent who warranted no respect—in order to hide from the real prospect of becoming one. The "psychological wage" of whiteness, which W.E.B. Du Bois famously identified in *Black Reconstruction* (1935) to explain what kept the white and black working classes apart, rested heavily on this formula, for no matter how far a white person fell in the competition with other whites, he could always look back and spot a dark face in his rearview mirror. Given the broad patterns of American politics since the late 1960s—from the success of the Republican "Southern Strategy," to the disaffection of northern working-class whites who abandoned the Democratic coalition in the 1970s and 1980s, to the racially inflected Tea Party movement and paranoid fears concerning a "Marxist," "Fascist," "Muslim," African American president—it would appear that an unfortunately high proportion of whites still subscribe to this way of thinking.

In his many essays on race and American identity, Ralph Ellison wrote artfully of what he called the democratic "chaos" that white Americans sought to avoid through their various projections onto African Americans. Today, this process might have more varied economic and social consequences than in the pre–civil rights era when Ellison gave it such eloquent codification, but the moral consequences have not changed very much at all. According to Ellison, these projections have at their root the cowardly avoidance of ethical responsibility to give shape to the self within a democratic culture. At its best, Ellison suggested, such a culture demands sincere engagement with diverse human possibility; at its worst, it cowers behind candy-coated fantasies of goodness already achieved and bounty with no consequence. As diligent and successful shapers of a way of life, African Americans have affirmed democratic possibility under the toughest circumstances by facing the ultimate threat of nothingness and bringing themselves into being, though they have also succumbed in countless ways to illusions stemming from the anger, despair, and resentment endemic to their social circumstance. Ellison's protagonist in the novel *Invisible Man* (1952) spends the larger part of the book living the false life of a black man on the make who takes his signals concerning who to be from whites, whose humanity he cannot clearly recognize for lack of facing his own. Just as whites project their desires onto him, he regards them as mere conduits to power, and thus as gods of a sort. His power fantasy engenders only weakness.[5]

The game of projection at the heart of race relations comes, according to Ellison, with a large portion of paranoia, as whites, subject to the identity confusion so basic to American life, know on some unconscious level that black skin forms the mystic writing pad of their own desires. Of course, blacks sense the same thing: that in important ways, white Americans, for all their apparent strength as a group, remain vulnerable and always a bit worried that the person behind the black mask must know their desires—and with that truth in hand, may well be putting one over on them. Today, in our post–civil rights period, a large part of this game occurs around the public drama of continuing black anger, the notion of "pulling the race card," and the seemingly bottomless need from whites for confirmation from blacks that racism no longer exists, or at the very least that they as individuals bear no visible trace of the unspeakable sin.

To this observation some might answer that black people no longer suffer from invisibility in the same way they did when Ellison penned his famous works. Over the past decades, although large portions of the black lower and working classes have remained poor—indeed, many have become even poorer—the black middle class has risen to unprecedented heights of professional achievement, inclusion in important institutions, and social exposure. Today, the appearance of black Americans in advertising and the media no longer surprises, nor do the images they portray necessarily reflect stereotypes. Some popular stars, such as Tiger Woods, whose multiracial background would not have spared him from being considered black in the pre–civil rights era, dwell in an apparent racial twilight zone that seems "neither black nor white, yet both."[6] Though the country remains highly segregated residentially and educationally, and intermarriage rates between blacks and whites show only incremental increases, surveys of white Americans reveal a continuing diminishment of overt racism rooted in ideas of biological inferiority. And the clincher of this case needs almost no mention: our president is an African American.

Yet these signs of progress seem to engender their opposite. The effort that our society has exerted to make advances in race relations has also served at times to reinforce the importance of race in our politics and to encourage new styles of racial identification. Nothing reflects this fact better than the effect of affirmative action policies, which have granted middle-class blacks unprecedented access to important institutions, but at the same time have led many whites to think in zero-sum terms about racial progress: a job given to a black American is one denied to a more qualified white. At times, even our celebrations of racial progress serve to reinforce boundaries between the races because they require us to reinscribe race discursively by employing it as a mode of classification. For example, a reporter commented after a speech by President Obama that, during the course of that address, he had forgotten Obama's race. No doubt his thought reflected that of many Americans of every description. Of course, this reporter's amazement at experiencing a supposedly raceless moment required him constantly to note, as Obama spoke, that he really was in the presence of the "other," but in a fashion both new and unapproachable because otherness itself was absent. In a sense, Obama had provided a moment for the reporter that exceeded the limits of his racial categories. But recognizing this fact required the evocation of a highly reified and essential form of blackness, a virtual thing in itself requiring almost no content. Though Obama did not "talk black" or "act black"—apparently, he did not even "look black" to this reporter—somehow, he was black, nonetheless.

Such are the confusions of our moment, emanations of an undigested past. In *Black Odyssey* (1977), a book that over the years has become a classic in Black Studies for its challenge to the progressive brand of American historiography, Nathan Huggins reaches back in his epilogue to wonder how the sprawling green visage of the new world first appeared to the twenty slaves aboard the fateful Dutch ship that lay off the shore of Jamestown in 1619.[7] In making this gesture, he parodies (to some extent) the final scene of F. Scott Fitzgerald's *The Great Gatsby* (1925), which famously reflects on the beauty and tragedy of the American insistence on remaining forever new. Though he does not say so directly, Huggins suggests that the powerful effect of Fitzgerald's famous passage, in all its tragic wisdom, depends in part on the exclusion of those early black captives, who also brought dreams with them, however muted by misfortune. While these dreams, and the efforts they engendered, would over generations play a great role in constituting the American experience, so would the attempts to exclude them or to play down their importance. Our nation has certainly made some progress on this record, but it has not arrived at the new narrative of the American experience that Huggins thought necessary to align American dreams with the events that have made us who we are. Race has marked American culture trenchantly, as it has marked the basic principles that we regard as raceless. Recognizing the full meaning of this thought will require a new narrative, indeed. In his last sentence, both in homage and in mild derision, Huggins quotes the famous last line of *Gatsby*, which still merits our deepest reflection: "So we beat on, boats against the current, borne back ceaselessly into the past."

Notes

1. On the connection between republicanism and slavery, see Edmund Morgan, *American Slavery, American Freedom: The Ordeal of Colonial Virginia* (New York: W. W. Norton, 1995), 363–390; also Edmund S. Morgan, "Slavery and Freedom: The American Paradox," *Journal of American History* 59, no. 1 (June 1972): 5–29.
2. Étienne Balibar, "Is There a 'Neo-racism'?," in *Race, Nation, Class*, by Étienne Balibar and Immanuel Wallerstein (London: Verso, 1991), 17–28.
3. See Noel Ignatiev, *How the Irish Became White* (New York: Routledge, 1995); David R. Roediger, *The Wages of Whiteness* (New York: Verso, 2007); and Matthew Frye Jacobson, *Whiteness of a Different Color* (Cambridge, MA: Harvard University Press, 1998).
4. Alexis de Tocqueville, *Democracy in America* (Chicago: University of Chicago Press, 2002), 302–391.
5. Ralph Ellison, *Invisible Man* (New York: Random House, 1995); Ralph Ellison, "Twentieth Century Fiction and the Mask of Humanity," in *Shadow and Act* (New York: Random House, 1995), 24–29, 41; see also, in the same volume, "Change the Joke and Slip the Yoke," 53.

6. This is the title of Werner Sollors's authoritative account of interracial literature in America; see Werner Sollors, *Neither Black nor White yet Both: Thematic Explorations of Interracial Literature* (Cambridge, MA: Harvard University Press, 1999).
7. Nathan Irvin Huggins, *Black Odyssey: The Afro-American Ordeal in Slavery* (New York: Random House, 1990), 243–244.

A Blue Note on Black American Literary Criticism and the Blues

All but abandoned by black audiences and seemingly locked in a suspended animation of commemoration—from remastered recordings of past artists to endless renditions of old standards at nationwide clubs devoted to its memory—the blues nevertheless enjoys an unprecedented vogue within the field of Black Studies. Though regarded with a certain doubt, or even disdain, among the majority of black thinkers before the 1970s for its low cultural, or even primitive, folk origins and its fundamentally apolitical posture, the blues enjoys an iconic status today as an almost unquestioned source of practical philosophical wisdom, artistic guidance, and contact with an increasingly remote yet distinctly black American past marked by slavery and legal segregation in the South. The names of artists and scholars over the past decades who have in one way or another pledged allegiance with the blues, praised its qualities, or mined its verses in various essays, poetry, drama, or fiction reads like a roll call of the best minds in the field. A very short list includes Alice Walker, Michael S. Harper, Gayl Jones, Shirley Anne Williams, Clarence Major, Cornel West, August Wilson, Toni Morrison, Angela Davis, Hazel Carby, Houston Baker, and Paul Beatty.[1]

Such prominent blues advocates and admirers have inspired many others of lesser renown to seed the journals with hundreds of essays examining reflections of the blues in a wide range of canonical authors, from the least "bluesy," such as Nella Larsen, Charles Chesnutt, and W.E.B. Du Bois, to authors who make direct reference to the blues, such as Langston Hughes, Ralph Ellison, and Toni Morrison. Reading this scholarly literature, which yields many important insights on how various writers conceived of the blues, one might nevertheless forget many important black authors like Walter White, Frank Yerby, or Jessie Fauset who show very little interest in the subject. It might also escape notice that an author so dedicated to the struggles of ordinary black people as Richard Wright, a native of blues capital Mississippi, could have such a horrible ear for the music that he could write in "King Joe," his own thirteen-stanza blues song about boxer Joe Louis, "Wonder what Joe Louis thinks when he's fighting a white man/Bet he thinks what I'm thinking because he wears a deadpan." Composed in 1941 at the suggestion of producer John Hammond and accompanied by Count Basie, Wright's awkward attempt at imitating the folk was sung with equal incompetence by actor and folk singer Paul Robeson. Of the stilted Robeson, Basie quipped politely, "The man certainly can't sing the blues" (Gussow 141). If the blues were the center of African American culture, as some contend, important figures like Wright and Robeson might well marginalize themselves through sheer badness.

Yet, given the generous parameters of current blues aesthetic criticism, these two rather un-bluesy figures might still qualify as members of a blues tradition just for the fact of the performance. Rather than evoking a specific history, particular songs, or the ability to produce or imitate them well, most current blues aesthetic criticism tends to reference the blues as a general sensibility or as an abstract "matrix" of values, concepts, and emotions that define black American cultural practice in general and ground black American literature in the world-making philosophy, linguistic practices, and musical traditions of ordinary blacks. Instead of actual blues songs, or their varied histories, blues aesthetic critics typically cite the general qualities of the music—its general formal features, its emphasis on nonlinearity, improvisation, loss, chance, turns of fate, and stories without sure conclusions—when characterizing how black American literary texts employ it as a foundation for expression. Because the blues possesses such features, and yet originated in the South as a type of music sung by blacks for blacks, it appears to balance perfectly a modern, or even postmodern, complexity with authentic racial origins. Thus, for many critics, it suggests a valuable conduit to the past, but one that avoids the loss of contemporary relevance that so often accompanies such journeys.

Although the use of the blues as a grounding paradigm for black American literature has reached an apogee of sorts in the post–civil rights era, the basic idea goes back more than eighty years. During the Harlem Renaissance, poets Langston Hughes and Sterling Brown sought to capture in the written word the power of black oral expression in poems that employed directly various formal elements of the blues.[2] From the 1940s through the 1960s, the blues received further theoretical elaboration as a philosophical and stylistic source for black literature in the works of Ralph Ellison and Albert Murray, who wrote trenchant essays concerning the existential and mythic meaning of the music as they employed it centrally as a resource in their fiction. Rather than opposition, both of these authors emphasized black American difference and survival within the context of a multiform and highly imperfect American democracy that victimized its black citizens even as they contributed incisively, and quite often invisibly, to its cultural depth.[3]

In *Blues People* (1963), a landmark text within the twentieth-century debate on the wider meaning of the blues, cultural nationalist poet Amiri Baraka (LeRoi Jones) ran directly against the inherently liberal formulations of Ellison and Murray by denying the essential Americanness of both black Americans and the blues. For Baraka, black Americans remained forever transplanted Africans, permanent aliens, or non-Americans, within the American cultural and political context, first for their Africanity, and second for the special culture that they formed in adjusting to the harsh terms of American racial oppression. Thus, he regarded the blues as the outgrowth of a resilient African inheritance and as evidence of continuing cultural resistance. One might wonder, therefore, how he might interpret Bessie Smith's seemingly patriotic sentiment in "Poor Man's Blues" (1928), as she pleads with the rich to recognize their dependence on the loyalty of the man farthest down.

> Poor man fought all the battles
> Poor man would fight again today
> Poor man fought all the battles
> Poor man would fight again today
> He would do anything you ask him
> In the name of the U.S.A.

Baraka might encounter similar difficulties with Huddie (Leadbelly) Ledbetter's enthusiastic embrace of the Allied war effort in "Hitler Song" (1942):

> We gonna tear Hitler down
> We gonna tear Hitler down
> We gonna tear Hitler down, someday
> We gonna bring him to the ground
> We gonna bring him to the ground someday.

We may debate whether the blues were, as Baraka contended, essentially African in form, but it makes little sense to deny that at times they could be all too American in substance.

Today, most blues aesthetic critics reject the racial essentialism of Baraka's classic book, but in emphasizing the blues as a kind of black American property many do skate on the edge of what they deny (Jones, *Blues People*). This appears clearly the case in Houston Baker's *Blues, Ideology, and African American Literature* (1984), a book that in many ways serves as a signal text for the discourse on literature and the blues throughout the post–civil rights era. When Baker characterizes the blues as a "vibrant network" or as a "multiplex enabling *script* in which African American discourse is inscribed" (4), he significantly abstracts the basic terms of *Blues People* seemingly to retain its more fundamental aim. In Baker's accounting, the blues performs the fundamental job of an essence, even as it floats in a conceptual hall of mirrors that deflects every attempt at definition (4). And where Baker's meaning appears clear, we may still wonder if it really does correspond with some of the most characteristic messages of the blues. At the top of his introduction, Baker quotes, along with Hegel's *Phenomenology of Spirit* and Baraka's *Dutchman*, the following lines from Robert Johnson's "Crossroad Blues":

> Standing at the Crossroads, tried to flag a ride
> Standing at the Crossroads, tried to flag a ride
> Ain't nobody seemed to know me, everybody passed me
> by. (1)

Baker goes on in the ensuing pages to define the blues as the product of a decentered subjectivity that always stands at a meeting of roads, or at the junction of a railroad line, "providing resonance for experience's multiplicities." "Singer and song never arrest transience," he says. "Instead they provide expressive equivalence for the juncture's ceaseless flux" (7). This appears to correspond reasonably well with the given quotation from "Crossroad Blues." Yet, quoted at a bit more length, Johnson's song invites a countervailing interpretation, even to Baker's many-sided claim:

> Mmm, the sun goin' down, boy, dark gon' catch me here.
> Oooo ooee, boy, dark gon' catch me here.
> I haven't got no lovin' sweet woman that love and feel
>   my care.
> You can run, you can run, tell my friend Poor Willie
>   Brown
> You can run, tell my friend, Poor Willie Brown
> Lord, that I'm standing at the crossroad, babe,
> I believe I'm sinkin' down. (Qtd. in Litwack 410)

A multiple subject may well stand at the crossroads in this song, but we may go along with historian Leon Litwack in acknowledging his fear of the dangers that he will inevitably meet standing in this unfortunate place at the wrong time (410). Poor Willie Brown was lynched, and the singer of this song trembles at the prospect himself. Rather than the tricky escape of the multiply-signifying trickster, "Crossroad Blues" evokes more centrally those problems in life that cannot be escaped, that must be faced, however much one wishes for the scene to change. Especially in the image of "sinkin' down" right in the center of a nexus, it recalls death, but with a dread appropriate to the idea of finality. Understandably, it also evokes the relatively static and conventional wish for warmth and understanding in the arms of a "sweet woman," again appropriate in part to depict the terror of the crossroads in the bold relief of tender and vaguely domestic associations. In this song, Johnson seems to say, perhaps in anticipation of interpreters like Baker who detect only his more trickster-ish and peripatetic inclinations, that even the most multiple of subjects must face fully the coldest disappointments of mortality.

Most artists and critics who have looked to the blues as a grounding discourse for black literature over the years have also tended to consider jazz for the same reasons. Yet, the blues has generally maintained a stronger association with vernacular traditions than jazz because of its emphasis on the spoken word and its deeper resemblance to poetry, storytelling, and the Southern folk context. Because of this, it has also carried with it an even stronger association with black authenticity. For many years, in fact, historians and critics tended to regard the blues as a primitive precursor of jazz rather than a different but related form of music. In addition, as jazz musicians employed difficult technical innovations, from the 1940s Bebop era to the present, to insulate their art from the encroachments of popular culture and amateurish imitation, the blues has gone in the opposite direction by mixing and melding with many forms of music, including jazz, gospel, country, and many others. Because of this tendency to meld, the blues has retained, along with its reputation for black authenticity, an association with the tastes of ordinary people, as opposed to the somewhat more avant-garde appeal of jazz.

Literary critics have never sat very comfortably with the more commercial side of blues history, even though they have tended to pay attention to the blues at the very times in which it has enjoyed its greatest commercial success. For example, Hughes and Brown explored the poetic potential of the blues during one of its legendary boom periods in the 1920s. Though Ellison's and Murray's careers spanned more than one blues vogue, their reflections on the nexus of music and black American literature originate partly in response to the

1940s blues revival on the left. And despite Baraka's claims for the separateness of black culture, his *Blues People* corresponds directly with the early days of the 1960s folk music movement, which spurred a renewed interest in the blues among young people across the United States. In other words, literary critics seem to see the greatest possibilities for the blues at the very times when everybody else does. Nevertheless, the intellectuals have tended to invest in the blues in opposition to shallow and artificial commercial products. Against the cheapening forces of commodification, they have generally held out for a pure or original form of the music against the more melded or mongrel creations of the marketplace, which have threatened to undermine the more ennobling and aura-conferring associations with the folk.

Despite the desires of intellectuals, the history of the blues remains inseparable from a restless commercialism and melding of multiple musical influences both among black musical styles and across racial lines. In short, the purest thing about this promiscuous musical form is its defiance of purity. The very forces that tended to stretch the blues toward more urban or melded expressions characteristically gave rise to countervailing demands for more rural or authentic representations of the music. Yet, even the most rural-seeming expressions of the blues always incorporated or directly referenced urban styles, which were distributed widely on records and on the radio. Over the years, blues performers typically adjusted to the diverse demands of their various audiences, whose changing needs across several periods of American race relations—from the era of segregation through two major waves of black migration to the North, through the civil rights movement—drove the desire for both novelty and a return to racial roots, in other words for both the line between the races and its continual violation.

Although the history of the blues resists almost every generalization commonly applied to it, we may pursue with caution a broad description of its major features without violating unduly its multifaceted character. The blues began as a fully developed musical form in the difficult days of the late nineteenth century as a product of the first generation of black Americans born in freedom. Emancipated as the result of the Civil War and guaranteed the rights of citizenship by a series of amendments to the Constitution passed soon after the war's bloody conclusion, these "New Negroes" lived the bitter reality of freedom denied at almost every turn.[4] Little wonder, then, that they would, among their many achievements, bring to full expression a cultural mode specifically tuned to the conveyance of intertwined joy and sorrow and illustrative of the discipline, toughness, and protean spirit necessary to find hidden bits of affirmation in a life circumstance that spoke most often in negative tones. In retrospect at least, it also does not surprise that this mode would depart from the main thrust of slave culture in focusing predominantly on subjective realities, that its artists would employ it constantly in coping with "the jagged grain of experience," or that it would speak to and for many black Americans both in the era of its invention and beyond.[5] Yet, the broad influence of the blues as a popular musical form in a nation addicted to a prevailing progressive perspective—in essence to the denial of every gesture of the blues—might still provoke astonishment, even among those most familiar with the details of its development as the root form of almost all current popular music from hard rock to rap.

As noted above, some blues critics prefer to emphasize its Africanity: its use of an African-derived three-line (AAB) twelve-bar form; its slurring and bending of notes; its stretching of musical instruments toward the expressive flexibility of the human voice; and its employment of shouts, falsetto, and guttural sounds to convey the inner feeling of the singer. Yet, a very good blues song may well have been written with the title "Africans Don't Have the Blues," in recognition of the complete absence of this musical form among those who provided some of its basic technical elements. Even Amiri Baraka agrees with this much in insisting that the blues could only have been invented in America. Though some early precursors of the blues did exist among slaves in the form of field shouts and work songs, they did not, for the most part, have the blues either, despite much sadness and travail. Notwithstanding its darker roots, the blues required the modernizing context of late nineteenth-century America for its invention. In this period, black Americans had become not only free, but also more secular and more individualistic, some might say more modern, than their predecessors (Levine 223).

Unlike earlier forms of black American song, which placed communal modes of performance at the center, the blues focused most prototypically on the personal revelations of an individual singer accompanied in most cases only by his own musical instrument. Nevertheless, the individualistic form of the blues made possible a powerful dynamic of audience identification because each listener could regard the revelations of the singer as his own, or alternately, see the singer as a focused instance of universal or representative human predicaments and emotions. To an extent, this required the audience to suspend the sense of distance between the act and the actor, even though every good blues singer understood quite well that success with an audience required her primarily to fulfill its needs, and to portray its experiences, through her own. Thus, standing alone, but often as the focus of a collective ritual, and using her instrument as the only source of response, but nevertheless constantly aware of her listeners, the classic blues singer could give the appearance of standing for the highest and most native powers of the naked soul facing the alternately exhilarating and disappointing events of this life solely through the creative use of its own resources, without otherworldly support. Rather than rely on God, or any outside source of comfort or deliverance, the self-reliant blues singer attempted to make suffering livable in part by entering into its folds and crevices. In some ways a rhythmic confessional, productive of a truth at times both terrible and exhilarating, the blues sought an enchantment of this life in all of its contradiction as it transformed prayerful and ecstatic religious moods into a secular but bracing and transportative alternative to religious doctrine and attitude. Thus, as it disavowed religion, and the spirituals, the blues incorporated them to great effect.

Though the blues focused most typically on the vicissitudes of emotion and circumstance around lost love, its thematic range encompassed a wide variety of everyday pains and pleasures that religious discourse either denounced or left unaddressed. Some observers, captured by the pseudo-sympathetic idea of the suffering black American—a liberal inversion of the happy slave stereotype—tended to confuse the blues with a simple singing of sadness, but even a glance at the range of subjects covered by this capacious art form makes such a view impossible. According to Leon Litwack, they included "travel (whether by foot or rail), the pain of loneliness and loss, faithlessness in love, sexual prowess, the meager rewards of labor, natural disasters (boll weevils and floods), dislocation, poverty, hypocritical preachers, escape through drink and drugs, the inequities of justice, the pervasiveness of color [prejudice], the satisfaction of vanquishing an adversary, the betrayal of expectations, [and] the imminence of violence and death" (454).

In short, the blues addressed the most quotidian worries of black Americans, from lamentation to celebration, from plaintive reflection on the odd turns of existence to the rhythmic and physical effort to stomp and belly rub the cares and tensions of life into temporary submission. And in the same way that the spirituals dominated the otherworldly cares of Sunday, the blues, as the party music of choice across the honky-tonks, work camps, and roadhouses of the black South, reigned in the more Dionysian atmosphere of the "Saturday Night Function."[6]

For this reason, religiously minded critics sometimes denounced the blues as the "devil's music" in recognition of its transgressive character. For somewhat different reasons, many upstanding middle-class blacks agreed. Afraid of the way that its downtrodden, work-rejecting singers and earthy songs appeared to confirm racial stereotypes, they tended to distance themselves from it. Rather than deny the negative claims of such detractors, many blues singers capitalized on them by constructing legends around the moral edge. For example, Robert Johnson, whose guitar-playing skills reputedly arose from a crossroads deal with Satan himself, inspired comparisons with such folkloric figures as the trickster and the conjure man. In a similarly inspired gesture, Leadbelly, the survivor of a shotgun blast and innumerable knife fights, billed himself as a singing criminal of sorts in general accordance with the mythic figure of the "badman" but also reflecting stereotypical accounts of black male aggression (F. Davis 164–169). Such stories gave substance to the wider association of the blues with racial authenticity and with the primitive and chaotic life on the bottom of American society, where naked, unregulated existence had a supposedly truer, more direct, and telling access to the soul in an unspoiled form. As it repelled guardians of convention, the transgressive reputation of the blues attracted those who felt shackled, victimized, or excluded by the standards that defined normative existence for most Americans. At its core, the blues challenged the efficacy of the work ethic, the privileging of mind over body, the rejection of the pleasures of this world for the promises of another, the expectation of inevitable progress, the comforts of linear narrative, and the desirability of conventional ideas of decency. Understood as a discourse out of the mainstream, it provided not only an alternative to the more self-conscious version of black American uplift ideology, but also a compelling answer to some of the most typical modes of American moralism, sentimentalism, and self-justification.

Although the blues incorporates important resistant gestures, such as the willingness to disclose thoughts and feelings frankly and fully despite racist suppression, ultimately it makes its greatest mark for its apolitical and anti-resistant posture. In *Stomping the Blues* (1976), cultural critic Albert Murray aptly employs literary critic Kenneth Burke's distinction between the Frame of Acceptance, which affirms the world with all of its various problems, and the Frame of Rejection, which protests against it, to distinguish the blues from modes of rhetoric that seek the transcendence of limitation rather than the exploitation of opportunities that a fractured world offers to experience moments of joy and freedom. In keeping with the basic spirit of the Frame of Acceptance, which according to Burke encompasses tragedy, comedy, humor, and the ode, the blues does not so much complain about the events of this life as it reports them, but in an artistic form that privileges improvisation and the potential for creative endeavor to reshape emotion. Although the blues relates many incidents that would seem to suggest protest, its appeal rests largely in not taking the bait. Nor does the blues typically enter into a political analysis of the troubled life, and even when it seems to, as in the songs that complain about the actions of bosses, it rarely suggests a political solution to the ills at hand. Instead, it emphasizes most the internal resources of the individual to affirm life, even in the darkest times (Murray, *Stomping* 251).

Despite this uplifting emphasis, the blues made a difficult match for the civil rights movement, which required uplifting songs that pointed to transcendent possibilities. For this reason, the anthems and marching songs of this era used the spirituals as their basis. Some black radicals of the 1960s, with Marxism and black nationalism rather than Christianity in mind, sometimes questioned directly the usefulness of the blues. Sounding a bit like folklorist Alan Lomax and other interpreters who saw in the blues only a recitation of suffering, nationalist Ron Karenga quipped: "Our creative motif must be revolution; all art that does not discuss or contribute to revolutionary change is invalid. That is why the 'blues' are invalid; they teach resignation" (38). Echoing this sentiment, and somewhat in opposition to the resistant reading of the blues asserted in *Blues People*, Baraka's protagonist in the play *Dutchman* (1960) states angrily, "If Bessie Smith had killed some white people, she wouldn't have needed that music" (1897).

After a long incubation period in the rural South, the blues first came formally to the stage in black minstrel shows and various other traveling variety shows around the turn of the century. Not long after, it came in distorted form to vaudeville and to Tin Pan Alley, at first as a variation on the "Coon Song"—a blackface comic ballad, sung in black dialect, accompanied by ragtime music, and usually amplifying one or more of the common black stereotypes, such as laziness, violence, and excessive appetite. Though men sang these songs, audiences preferred to hear them sung by white female "coon shouters" such as Sophie Tucker and May Irwin, who used the black mask as a cover of sorts for delving into risqué themes. As the popularity of the blues became apparent in the early 1920s, Tin Pan Alley began to produce a long series of "white" blues songs such as Jerome Kern's "Left All Alone Blues" (1920), George and Ira Gershwin's "Yankee Doodle Blues" (1922), and Richard Rodgers and Lorenz Hart's "Atlantic Blues" (1926), which offered some of the thematic husk of the blues while leaving out its formal musical kernel (Douglas 393).

In tandem with the general diffusion of the blues in American popular culture in this period, white popular music stars such as Fannie Brice and Libby Holman became famous for blues-based "torch" songs with titles like "My Man" and "Moanin' Low." Ironically, Mamie Smith's "Crazy Blues," the recording credited with starting the 1920s blues craze and opening up the market for "race" records, or records made for black consumers, resembled these torch songs much more than it reflected the core musical features of the blues. In fact, this song, written for the financially strapped Okeh record label by black vaudeville performer Perry Bradford, and originally offered to "coon shouter" Sophie Tucker, became a hit mostly because of the stamp of racial authenticity that the skin color of Smith, and her Harlem-based Jazz Hounds band, provided for working-class black migrants to the North, who wanted to purchase music explicitly by and about black people. Apparently, for these working-class blacks, "Crazy Blues" was blues enough, however bastardized by the attempt at crossover appeal (Douglas 391).

"Crazy Blues" sold over one million copies in its first year and two million total, opening the way for such blues women as Ma Rainey, Bessie Smith, Alberta Hunter, Ida Cox, and Ethel Waters to record innumerable "race" records for Paramount and Columbia, and for two short-lived black-owned labels, Black Swan and Black Patti, which brought the Harlem Renaissance dream of black-owned and black-supported cultural institutions to the then infant record industry. These early queens of the blues, who generally dressed to the nines, assumed the role of divas, never played instruments, and tended toward a "show business" presentation of their music, leaned more toward the melding of the blues with jazz, ragtime, and popular forms characteristic of the urban blues. Years later, when the tastes of fans and historians of the blues would emphasize the importance of folkloric purity, or the overhauls and guitar approach to the blues, the reputations of these women would recede into near invisibility.[7] In the past decades, they have been resurrected as heroes by such black feminist writers as Angela Davis and Hazel Carby, who regard them as resisters of race, class, and gender oppression. To a great extent, this interpretation has succeeded in correcting the record, though it appears at its weakest as an account of what the blues women actually sang about. In keeping with their identity as blues singers, and with the understandable desire to make money, they dwelled largely on "sweet daddies," "aggravatin' poppas," and otherwise oversexed black men, whom they alternately pledged to leave, shoot, or love all night long. Thus, they reflected in more benign fashion some of the key themes of the white female "coon shouters," who also played to audiences that wanted to hear transgressive and earthy female voices taunt and tickle as they defied conventional rules of acceptable feminine behavior.

As literary critic Ann duCille points out, feminist claims of oppositional sexual agency in the lyrics of blues women come up against serious limits in light of the traditional stereotypes of black female supersexuality that these otherwise inspiring figures often enthusiastically volunteered to mimic ("Blues Notes on Black Sexuality: Jessie Fauset and Nella Larsen" 427–428). Yet, in the most extremely sexual lyrics by the blues women it might be possible to discern an attempt at liberation that goes admirably beyond the limits of the relatively prim contemporary feminism that seeks to contain them within the staid confines of heroism. On this score, the relatively unsung queen of the "dirty blues," Lucille Bogan, a performer of narrow expressive range who specialized in songs glorifying sex and prostitution, provides a good case in point. Bogan's graphic and little-known "Shave 'Em Dry" (1935) deserves extensive quotation, in part because it gets quoted rarely, and for the sake of sheer fun:

> I got nipples on my titties, big as the end of my thumb,
> I got somethin' between my legs'll make a dead man
> come, [. . .]
> Want you to grind me baby, grind me until I cry. And I'll
> give you somethin'
> baby, swear it'll make you cry
> I'm gon' turn back my mattress, and let you oil my springs
> I want you to grind me daddy, 'till the bell do ring
> Oh daddy want you to shave 'em dry,
> Oh great God daddy, if you can't shave 'em baby won't you
> try?
> Now if fuckin' was the thing, that would take me to
> heaven,
> I'd be a fuckin' in the studio, till the clock strike eleven,
> Oh daddy, daddy shave 'em dry,
> I would fuck you baby, honey I'd make you cry.
> Now your nuts hang down like a damn bell snapper,
>
> And your dick stands up like a steeple,
> Your goddamn ass-hole stands open like a church door
> And the crabs walk in like people. [. . .]
>
> A big sow gets fat from eatin' corn,
> And a pig gets fat from suckin',
> Reason you see this whore, fat like I am,
> Great God, I got fat from fuckin'. [. . .]

My back is made of whalebone,
And my cock is made of brass,
And my fuckin' is made for workin' men's two dollars,
Great God, round to kiss my ass.

Besides its uninhibited language and exuberant comic tone, this song, like so many "dirty blues" sung by both men and women, liberates mainly because the singer adores sex and thus represents a deep human desire without caring about the consequences. In this way, she takes her listener on a transgressive, and in some ways emancipative, journey. The embrace of stereotype, so often feared within the black American intellectual tradition, helps in this case to produce the overall effect of freedom. Comparing herself both to an inanimate object (a bed) and to animals, the singer proudly calls herself a whore as she seems to tell anyone who does not like it to "kiss her sex-loving ass." All the while, in a gesture that reflects sexual equality as much as the storied bittersweetness of the blues tradition, she commands her partner to make her cry as she promises to do the same to him. Yet, as she simultaneously taunts, exhorts, pleads, brags, and promises, she also appears at times to stand above her partner in a delightfully alternating sexual play that makes use of a range of emotions. The rather exaggerated manly impression of her partner's sex organs seems more the result of her own powers than his. Proud of her uncommon accomplishment as a whore, she accepts the money of working men who pay most of what they have just to get in the vicinity of her prize, which calls them into an experiential realm beyond the consequential aims of economics or politics. In her "dirty" song, Bogan ranks release, and the infinity of the moment, above the timeworn cares of everyday life. In this sense, she stands at the crossroads, but perhaps in a way that makes her memory hard for many scholars to mine fully.

The rise of a black urban market for the blues, created in large part by the success of the blues women, provided the impetus for Paramount to record Blind Lemon Jefferson, a partially blind itinerant native of Texas who sold and recorded as many blues records between 1926 and 1929 as Bessie Smith, Ma Rainey, or any of his other female counterparts. Jefferson's commercial success as a country blues singer and master guitarist motivated record companies to send representatives to the rural regions of the South to find authentic bluesmen they might market to both blacks and whites, who desired "originals" for related but different reasons (F. Davis 95–97, 169). New black migrants to the North enjoyed hearing music that reminded them of home, though they sometimes rejected country blues for jazz and popular music for the same reasons. Albeit whites in the 1920s listened mainly to "white" blues torch songs and Tin Pan Alley blues facsimiles, these blues-lite productions sometimes whetted their appetites for the "real thing." In searching the South for new talent, record companies hoped to exploit this opportunity.

The onset of the Depression all but destroyed opportunities for blues women, as it undermined sales for the fledgling record industry. Yet, such peripatetic bluesmen as Charlie Patton and Robert Johnson, individual performers who wandered about the South playing wherever people could collectively contribute a few dollars, continued to survive and develop their art in spite of the times. In many ways, the future of the blues would belong to these male performers, not just because of their skill or their gender, but because they survived to be recorded during an era that everyone associates with hard times and twisted fate. For the most part, later blues performers would cite them as seminal influences even as blues music developed in more urban and melded directions during the 1940s and 1950s (F. Davis 80–86). Oddly, these highly skilled male performers, who constituted a very exclusive elite group among black Southerners of their day, still represent for many current listeners the quintessence of romantic folkishness in musical form. Partly, this has to do with the strong element of haunting tragedy and violence that suffuses their music, along with the emphasis on masterful guitar technique that marked their Mississippi Delta version of the blues. More than other blues singers, these male singers from the deepest South corroborate best those interpretations of the blues that emphasize existential themes, that seek a certain authenticity through suffering, or envision a road back to Africa through the Mississippi Delta, where some believe that black American cultural memory reaches back the farthest.[8]

Today, the blues enjoys a revival of sorts, mainly among white audiences, due mostly to CD releases throughout the 1990s of the music of singers like Robert Johnson and to the rise of "roots" music, which also includes folk, reggae, and other traditional forms that provide an adult alternative to overproduced, market-oriented recordings made for youth. In some ways, this new market for the blues repeats the pattern of blues revivals in the 1940s, where the left became enamored with the blues as an organic expression of the downtrodden, and in the 1960s, where college students turned to folk music as an alternative to rock-and-roll, itself ironically a child of the blues (F. Davis 206–211). Despite its supposedly countercultural aims, and somewhat in keeping with earlier blues revivals, today's "roots" music movement has enabled a highly market-oriented packaging of the blues since the 1980s, evident in such standardized corporate products as the House of Blues restaurant chain, the B. B. King Blues Club chain, and several blues-themed movies, including *The Blues Brothers* (1980) and *The Blues Brothers 2000* (1998), which made comic actor Dan Aykroyd richer than even the most legendary blues singers. Purists may regard such tributes to the blues as sure evidence of demise, yet in another way they reflect a long history of white appreciation and copying of the blues from vaudeville to the present, a process central to the development of the music and productive itself of a wide range of creditable creative effort. In this regard, at least, the blues does live on, even if this life appears at times a desiccated shell filled with nostalgic renderings of old standards, endlessly recited to accompany an often sentimental crossing of an increasingly unclear post–civil rights era line between the races.

To add to the case for demise, as mentioned above, black audiences have for the most part abandoned the blues, though they do enjoy such blues-derived music as soul, rap, and rhythm and blues, which emphasize the more ecstatic, polyrhythmic, love-, sex-, braggadocio-, and crime-obsessed themes of the blues tradition over its more tragically introspective "jagged grain" and "trouble in mind" dimensions. The reasons for this seem clear. As the years pass, fewer black Americans can recall personal memories linked to northern migration, and thus fewer need a form of music to remind them of "home." Also, to borrow from Albert Murray's nomenclature, the civil rights movement inspired among black Americans a much deeper embrace of the Frame of Rejection, or the sense that the race problem could and should be overcome through direct opposition. Even in the post–civil rights era, where organized protest has all but died, the faith among blacks in transcendent solutions remains strong, though it has shifted in a more privatized and commodified direction, toward the realms of individual expression and pursuit of the good life in material terms. Although many problems remain, therefore, the blues, conceived of as a method for making a troubled life livable by entering into its terms, no longer addresses the predominant way most black Americans think of their needs, though a simple glance below the poverty line or into the racially skewed population of a prison block might suggest to an outside observer the continuing relevance of a blues sensibility.

The same general forces that have led to a waning of tragic blues sensibility among black Americans may also signal the end of black American literature. According to literary critic Kenneth W. Warren in *What Was African American Literature?* (2011), the idea of a specifically black American literary tradition with deep cultural referents, special literary techniques, and coherent lines of authorial descent has always served as a cultural accompaniment of the political struggle for black American freedom and equality from the Harlem Renaissance through the civil rights movement. Although they have argued mightily concerning the specific direction that resistance to racism ought to take, literary critics of this tradition have generally endeavored to demonstrate black American intellectual capability as they have provided ideological structures suggesting the image of a single people with a common destiny. For much of black American history, such ideas seemed practically necessary, even if they did not capture every nuance of class difference or ethnic and racial diversity. Yet the post–civil rights era appears more than ever to challenge the old faith in black Americans' unity. The material and spiritual divide between middle- and lower-class black Americans grows daily, as it increases for all Americans. Especially for middle-class blacks, the social line between the races grows murkier as young people who have no personal memory of past racial struggles interact within dynamic spheres of interracial contact. In response to such trends, some thinkers prefer, in the spirit of progress, to evoke the wonder of a post-racial era, but in doing so they wishfully ignore the continuing impact of race in American life, whose meaning propagates in every direction. Nevertheless, the new complexity of American race relations should provoke reflection on whether racial problems can find their solution in a resistance movement aimed at gaining rights for a single unified group.

According to Warren's provocative book, such realities may well have ended altogether the need for an African American literature, even one grounded in a discourse so many-sided as the blues. Indeed, the entire idea of grounding a literary tradition at all might be regarded as an ideological vestige of a bygone era. Of course, this does not mean the end of studying literature by black Americans, nor the literature about them. For this, we do not need the idea of a literary tradition with a capital *T*. The racial past brims with uncomfortable ironies, unexpected continuities, and unsettling discontinuities. It offers no sure answers and no single source of wisdom or comfort. Much of its value inheres within the complex tangles that have characterized human connection within the context of oppressive realities and relationships. By studying them we may only hope to gain a bit of distance from our own most comfortable racial complexes—a blue thought to conclude a blue note on black American literature and the blues.

Notes

1. For good summaries of recent discussions of African American literature and the blues, see Schreiber 472–473; Lock and Murray, "You've Got to Be Jazzistic." A very short list of important post–civil rights publications on the blues and African American literature includes Henderson; Williams; G. Jones 195–196; Schultz; Garon; Soitos; duCille, "Blues Notes on Black Sexuality: Sex and the Texts of Jessie Fauset and Nella Larsen" 418–422.
2. The blues appears in one way or another throughout Brown's verse. See Brown, *Collected Poems*. See also Brown, "The Blues

as Folk Poetry" 551; Rowell; and Sanders. For Hughes, see *Collected Poems of Langston Hughes*, here the poems from his first two collections, *The Weary Blues* (1926) and *Fine Clothes to the Jew* (1927). Also see Hughes, "Songs Called the Blues" 145; and Tracy.

3. Ralph Ellison's best and most famous statements on the blues occur in his novel *Invisible Man* and are spread throughout two books of essays, *Shadow and Act* and *Going to the Territory*. See especially "Richard Wright's Blues," *Shadow and Act* 77–94. Major works on the blues by Albert Murray include *Stomping the Blues*, *The Hero and the Blues*, and a novel, *Train Whistle Guitar*. Also see Callahan.
4. The term "New Negro" originated as a description for black slaves just arrived from Africa. It reappeared as a name for the first generation of blacks born after slavery. In the 1920s it resurfaced as a name for the more militant black attitude that arose after World War I and the black migration to the North.
5. The "jagged grain" reference is from an often quoted sentence in Ralph Ellison's "Richard Wright's Blues": "The blues is an impulse to keep the painful details and episodes of a brutal experience alive in one's aching consciousness, to finger its jagged grain, and to transcend it, not by the consolation of philosophy but by squeezing from it a near-tragic, near-comic lyricism" (*Shadow and Act* 78).
6. I take the term "Saturday Night Function" from Albert Murray's *Stomping the Blues*, where he contrasts the blues with the church, which dominated Sunday (24; see also 33–54; and Litwack 450).
7. Carby; A. Davis; see also Harrison; F. Davis 80–86.
8. See, for example, Ferris; Palmer.

Works Cited

Baker, Houston A. *Blues, Ideology, and African American Literature: A Vernacular Theory*. Chicago: University of Chicago Press, 1984. Print.

Baraka, Amiri (LeRoi Jones). *Dutchman. The Norton Anthology of African American Literature.* Ed. Henry Louis Gates Jr. et al. New York: Norton, 1997. 1885–1899. Print.

Bogan, Lucille. "Shave 'Em Dry." *Shave 'Em Dry: The Best of Lucille Bogan.* Columbia/Legacy, 2004. CD.

Brown, Sterling A. "The Blues as Folk Poetry." *The Jazz Cadence of American Culture.* Ed. Robert G. O'Meally. New York: Columbia University Press, 1998. 540–551. Print.

———. *The Collected Poems of Sterling Brown.* Ed. Michael S. Harper. Evanston, IL: Triquarterly, 1996. Print.

Callahan, John, ed. *Trading Twelves: The Selected Letters of Ralph Ellison and Albert Murray.* New York: Vintage, 2001. Print.

Carby, Hazel. "'It Jus' Be Dat Way Sometime': The Sexual Politics of Women's Blues." *Unequal Sisters: A Multicultural Reader in U.S. Women's History.* Ed. Ellen Carol Du Bois and Vikki L. Ruiz. London: Routledge, 1990. 238–249. Print.

Davis, Angela Y. *Blues Legacies and Black Feminism: Gertrude "Ma" Rainey, Bessie Smith and Billie Holliday.* New York: Vintage, 1999. Print.

Davis, Francis. *The History of the Blues: The Roots, the Music, the People.* New York: Hyperion, 1995. Print.

Douglas, Ann. *Terrible Honesty: Mongrel Manhattan in the 1920s.* New York: Farrar, 1995. Print.

duCille, Ann. "Blues Notes on Black Sexuality: Sex and the Texts of Jessie Fauset and Nella Larsen." *Journal of the History of Sexuality* 3.3 (1993): 418–444. Print.

———. "Blues Notes on Black Sexuality: Sex and the Texts of the Twenties and Thirties." *The Coupling Convention: Sex, Text, and Tradition in Black Women's Fiction.* By duCille. New York: Oxford University Press, 1993. 66–85. Print.

Ellison, Ralph. *Going to the Territory.* 1986. New York: Vintage, 1995. Print.

———. *Invisible Man.* 1952. New York: Vintage, 1995. Print.

———. *Shadow and Act.* 1964. New York: Vintage, 1995. Print.

Ferris, William. *Blues from the Delta*. Cambridge, MA: Da Capo, 1988. Print.

Garon, Paul. *Blues and the Poetic Spirit*. Rev. ed. San Francisco: City Lights, 1996. Print.

Gussow, Adam. "'Fingering the Jagged Grain': Ellison's Wright and the Southern Blues Violences." *Boundary* 30.2 (2003): 137–155. Print.

Harrison, Daphne Duval. *Black Pearls: Blues Queens of the 1920s*. New Brunswick, NJ: Rutgers University Press, 1988. Print.

Henderson, Stephen E. "The Blues as Black Poetry." *Callaloo* 16.3 (1982): 22–30. Print.

Hughes, Langston. *The Collected Poems of Langston Hughes*. Ed. Arnold Rampersad. New York: Vintage, 1995. Print.

———. "Songs Called the Blues." *Phylon* 2.2 (1941): 143–145. Print.

Johnson, Robert. "Crossroad Blues." *Robert Johnson: The Complete Recordings*. Sony, 1990. CD.

Jones, Gayl. *Liberating Voices: Oral Tradition in African American Literature*. Cambridge, MA: Harvard University Press, 1991. Print.

Jones, LeRoi (Amiri Baraka). *Blues People: Negro Music in White America*. 1963. New York: Harper, 2002. Print.

Karenga, Ron. "Black Cultural Nationalism." *The Black Aesthetic*. Ed. Addison Gayle. Garden City, NY: Doubleday, 1971. 32–38. Print.

Leadbelly. "Hitler Song." *Bourgeois Blues: Lead Belly Legacy*. Vol. 2. Smithsonian Folkways, 1993. CD.

Levine, Lawrence W. *Black Culture and Black Consciousness: Afro-American Folk Thought from Slavery to Freedom*. New York: Oxford University Press, 1977. Print.

Litwack, Leon. *Trouble in Mind: Black Southerners in the Age of Jim Crow*. New York: Knopf, 1998. Print.

Lock, Graham, and David Murray, eds. *Thriving on a Riff: Jazz and Blues Influences in African American Literature and Film*. New York: Oxford University Press, 2009. Print.

———. “You’ve Got to Be Jazzistic.” Introduction. Locke and Murray 1–18.

Murray, Albert. *The Hero and the Blues*. 1973. New York: Vintage, 1996. Print.

———. *Stomping the Blues*. 1976. Cambridge, MA: Da Capo, 2000. Print.

———. *Train Whistle Guitar*. 1974. New York: Vintage, 1998. Print.

Palmer, Robert. *Deep Blues: A Musical and Cultural History of the Mississippi Delta*. New York: Penguin, 1982. Print.

Rowell, Charles H. “Let Me Be with Ole Jazzbo: An Interview with Sterling Brown.” *Callaloo* 21.4 (1998): 789–809. Print.

Sanders, Mark A. *Afro-Modernist Aesthetics and the Poetry of Sterling A. Brown*. Athens: University of Georgia Press, 1999. Print.

Schreiber, Andrew Joseph. “Jazz and the Future Blues: Toni Morrison’s Urban Folk Zone.” *Modern Fiction Studies* 52.2 (2006): 470–494. Print.

Schultz, Elizabeth. “To Be Black and Blue: The Blues Genre in Black American Autobiography.” *Kansas Quarterly* 7.3 (1975): 81–96. Print.

Smith, Bessie. “Poor Man’s Blues.” *Bessie Smith: The Complete Recordings*. Sony, 1993. CD.

Soitos, Stephen. *The Blues Detective: A Study of African American Detective Fiction*. Amherst: University of Massachusetts Press, 1996. Print.

Tracy, Steven. *Langston Hughes and the Blues*. Urbana: University of Illinois Press, 1988. Print.

Warren, Kenneth W. *What Was African American Literature?* Cambridge, MA: Harvard University Press, 2011. Print.

Williams, Sherley Anne. “The Blues Roots of Contemporary Afro-American Poetry.” *Chant of Saints: A Gathering of Afro-American Literature, Art, and Scholarship*. Ed. Michael Harper and Robert B. Stepto. Urbana: University of Illinois Press, 1979. 123–135. Print.

Of Mr. W.E.B. Du Bois and Others

Though he rose only occasionally to the highest heights of literary sublimity, and he never penned a single word of good poetry, W.E.B. Du Bois nonetheless stands above all other intellectual figures as the strong poet of the African American experience. As Harold Bloom relates on the way to coining this term as a keyword toward an understanding of the mysterious agony of influence experienced by the great writers of Western literature, who depend for their very name on surpassing and thereby succeeding other great writers, such figures threaten their best readers with a kind of intellectual death, even as the terms they offer provide a seemingly emancipatory mapping of otherwise unknowable terrains of experience. Du Bois succeeds in achieving this effect not only for what he wrote, but also for his authorship of an exemplary life, one lived over the course of nearly one hundred years, bridging two great periods of racial upheaval, from the tense and violent, yet hope-filled period following the Civil War to the anxious, embattled, and still violent era of the civil rights movement. Over the course of these years, which he traversed as both a leader of his people and as their most abiding intellectual voice—one that encompassed history, sociology, political science, high and low literature, cultural criticism, oratory, journalism, propaganda, song, prayer, and nearly every possible thought that one could think about the meaning of race within an ever-unfolding modernity—Du Bois wrote most centrally as a way of fighting, and of calling other African Americans over to the arduous path of dignity through resistance. Of himself he asserted in his 1940 autobiography *Dusk of Dawn* (in whose subtitle he characterized his own life as the very unfolding of a race concept): "I think I may say without boasting that in the period from 1910 to 1930 [roughly his period as editor of the NAACP journal *The Crisis*], I was a main factor in revolutionizing the attitude of the American Negro toward caste. My stinging hammer blows made Negroes aware of themselves, confident of their possibilities and determined in self-assertion. So much so that today common slogans among the Negro people are taken bodily from the words of my mouth."

Du Bois may well have been right in this, although one imagines African Americans managing a fairly robust hatred for their place in American society without stealing from his enchantingly animated prose. Nevertheless, the main thrust of this self-observation rings true, even for us today, for Du Bois remains one of the sources for conceiving of African American life as a resistant and embattled condition, one that will find its ultimate solution in a robust racial politics carried forward by a battle-ready, self-recognizing, and self-transcending people. Yet in articulating this message in different ways over the years, Du Bois, like most engaged thinkers of long standing, encompassed an astonishing range of seeming contradictions. But even these tend to contribute to his historic stature. As he followed a generally leftward (some might say more radical) trajectory that took him from the Berkshire Hills, Harvard, and Atlanta in his early years to Nkrumah's Ghana at his death, he somehow made it possible for liberals, Marxists, post-Marxists, nationalists, Afrocentrists, pragmatists, culturalists and materialists, atheists and theists, the violent and the nonviolent, to claim him proudly as a forebear. Like a biblical patriarch, it may be said that Du Bois fathered many children, who currently still scramble to claim his inheritance along with the blessings that come with it. He thus captures many, so to speak, for having said and done so much so well, and for so long. Yet in receiving his multifarious inheritance, we might still wonder what price it brings. What are the limits of our Du Boisian currency?

Admittedly, this formulation of Du Bois as a seminal influence may appear to underplay to some extent the amount of disagreement that surrounds his figure, both now and in the past. During the 1920s, for example, the very heart of the period that Du Bois cites in the above quotation as most shaped by his influence, the Jamaican nationalist Marcus Garvey denounced him as a light-skinned bourgeois traitor to his people; A. Philip Randolph and Chandler Owen of the socialist *Messenger* magazine took an unmistakable joy in categorizing him as an old man and as a stalwart force among the shuffling "old crowd Negroes," whose extinction, they asserted, would advance African American politics beyond its fatal and submissive compromise with capitalism, war, imperialism, and the belief in race as a legitimate category in the classification of humanity. In the same era, artists of the Harlem Renaissance such as Claude McKay, Langston Hughes, Zora Neale Hurston, and Wallace Thurman found themselves at odds with Du Bois's narrowly propagandistic and sanitized "best foot forward" version of African American art, which embraced group expressivism while somehow missing entirely the expressive energy of jazz, the blues, African American dance, language, and folklore—seemingly the most powerful examples of black spirit or soul that the age had to offer. Yet, the terms for such anti–Du Boisian criticism could well have derived from the philosophy of the man himself. The same might be said of many current attempts to slip the Du Boisian yoke, as Robert Gooding-Williams points out in his *The Shadow of Du Bois*, a book that seeks an alternative model for black American politics in the views of Frederick Douglass as it announces in no uncertain terms the continuing power of the Du Boisian paradigm in guiding conceptualizations of black American politics, even at this late date, when so many of the basic conditions of African American life appear a world apart from the segregated realities that drove Du Bois's best known formulations.

Although we may quarrel, as many interpreters have, as to whether Du Bois altered his fundamental conceptualization of the race problem or simply changed his emphasis in his late career, the main elements of the paradigm with which he has been most closely associated receive their crystalline expression in *The Souls of Black Folk* (1903), a work pieced out of essays that he published in his late twenties and early thirties. Most centrally, the perspective of *Souls* stands on five pillars. First, Du Bois characterizes African Americans as a people sharing a group ethos rooted both in slavery and in Africa that they must bring into modern expression over the course of their struggle in America. This ethos is in the end the difference that makes a difference about them. It provides the wellspring of unity, an animating telos, the key to true consciousness, and the ultimate "So what?" of their politics, which is the force through which they bring themselves into being as a world-historical people endowed with a special gift for humanity.

Second, Du Bois characterizes African Americans as possessing a double or split consciousness due to American racism, which excludes them violently, forcing them to view themselves falsely, as if from outside of themselves, thus undermining their ability to value and to invest effort in themselves for their own sake. Though this double consciousness also affords them "second sight" or the ability to see their oppressors in some ways better than their oppressors see themselves, it must nonetheless be superseded by a more integrated, and thus truer, melding of its two parts.

Third, Du Bois insists that in order to realize themselves most fully, African Americans must carry on a concerted struggle against every manifestation of racism, thus enhancing the conditions for mutual recognition with whites and an end to debilitating double consciousness, which stands at odds with the synthesis of Negro and American souls, of the premodern and the modern, so to speak, that constitutes their promise as a people.

Fourth, Du Bois demands that the African Americans most closely familiar with modernity, the educated middle class that he calls "the Talented Tenth," lead the struggle against racism in part by uplifting the comparatively ignorant mass of their people, who in spite of possessing the most authentic raw material of group spirit, nonetheless succumb to the corruption of double consciousness, as they lack sufficient familiarity with modern consciousness to seek the kind of power or self-knowledge that might set them on the proper track to end their fecklessness and fulfill their destiny. As the Talented Tenth provides political and moral guidance to the masses, its members must remain cognizant that their uplifting duty to the less fortunate members of their group provides their only route to transcendence, recognition, and self-realization so long as America remains racist and they remain black. Their effort to transform the masses therefore also transforms them as they lead a resistance struggle against racism and attempt to rearticulate the black culture in modern terms.

Fifth, and last, the charge of the Talented Tenth also sets out the task of the black intellectual, who in Du Bois's rendering serves as the spearhead of knowledge gathering concerning the hidden meaning of being an African American, thus serving as a sensitive interpreter and promoter and, in another sense, a fulfiller of African American self-consciousness and destiny. Given Du Bois's framework, this task of gathering and interpreting has inherent political meaning not only because it makes African Americans more modernistically aware of themselves, but also because it sets up the possibility of at least some whites seeing them with altered eyes. The role of the intellectual in documenting, gathering, sensitively interpreting, and rearticulating African American experience for the sake of a politics of recognition goes hand in hand with his other role as public voice, or perhaps as a propagandist, striking hammer blows against racism, again in the effort to undermine the conditions of double consciousness and to speed the unfolding of African American destiny.

I am sure that some of you have noticed that I have angled my description of Du Bois's approach in *Souls* to emphasize the devotion of this text to an ideal of African American empowerment, a point that can get lost in readings that get too involved in its masterful expressive dimensions, or too monumental in locating the sources of the master's words and concepts, especially interpretations that regard Du Bois's efforts to describe how it feels to be black as a kind of point in itself. It is well to note that the author of *Souls* remains in some ways the youthful admirer of Bismarck who praised the German leader in his valedictory address at Fisk for the use of force in uniting, and thus modernizing, "a bickering people"—a trick that the young Du Bois would not have minded applying in the case of African Americans. On this point, we might acknowledge a certain truth in political scientist William Strickland's description of Du Bois on the Schomburg Center website as "the Prime Minister of the state we never had." Or, more on the comic side of this issue, we might notice journalist George S. Schuyler's nearly perfect sardonic naming of the Du Bois character in the 1931 satirical classic *Black No More* as Shakespeare Agamemnon Beard—the poet who "sits with Shakespeare," the warrior/king who leads feckless far-flung battles for questionable ends, and the somewhat odd-looking Germanophile black professor. Of course, Schuyler meant to evoke laughter in crafting this portrait, and to his credit, Du Bois not only found his caricature humorous, but he signed his favorable review of the book with Schuyler's cleverly crafted moniker.

Of course, humorous reflection on Du Bois's desire to fashion his people into an effective and united political force can only go so far, not just because Du Bois so often preferred a mask of solemnity, but also because so much about his perspective derives from an attempt to face directly and seriously the often brutish violence of American race relations. For the young Du Bois, this violence manifested itself palpably not only in the overtly racist terms of the segregated social order of his day, but in two events, both occurring in 1899, that brought racial hatred to his doorstep. The first, a gruesome lynching of a black farmer named Sam Hose, who shot and killed a white farmer over a debt, not only brought home the visceral racial hatred of southern whites, who not only killed and burned and dismembered Hose, but also made Du Bois doubt the efficacy of his own efforts to save and uplift the race through honest scholarship and high ideals. According to biographer David Levering Lewis, when Du Bois was told on his way to deliver a letter of protest to the editor of the *Atlanta Constitution* that a butcher in downtown Atlanta displayed Hose's burned knuckles in the window of his shop, the cane-carrying, white-gloved avatar of the Talented Tenth simply returned home, letter still in hand, to contemplate the ineffectiveness of social science conceived as a force for positive social change.

The second violent event of 1899 involved the death of Du Bois's two-year-old son Burghardt from diphtheria, an unnecessary and spirit-breaking event in part due to Du Bois's workaholic negligence, but mostly the result of a shortage of competent black doctors in Atlanta and the willingness of white southern doctors to see African Americans die rather than suffer the humiliation (and the implication of human sympathy) involved in treating them. In a sense one could say that the child died a victim of the racist order of things, a fact that led Du Bois to a range of broad and guilt-laced reflections on race and group survival, and the seeming hopelessness of hope for black Americans, in "On the Passing of the First Born," a chapter of *Souls* whose biblically inspired title points, in its reference to Exodus, to a potential deliverance for the group despite the forces of ethnic cleansing and Social Darwinism that appeared to threaten even the most humble ideas of an African American destiny. As Susan Mizruchi points out in her chapter on Du Bois in *The Science of Sacrifice*, the social scientifically underwritten idea of African Americans as a dying people, as a sacrifice of sorts for the emergence of an ever more modern and ever whiter America haunts *Souls*, even as Du Bois makes his case for the world-historical gift that lies hidden within the inner depths of his people. Perhaps most chillingly, this idea of racial sacrifice served as a device, evident in ritual events like the Sam Hose lynching, for placing whiteness and white community on a transcendent, and even innocent, basis in the minds of its possessors—an all-too-familiar marriage of the barbaric and the modern that expressed itself as comfortably in racial slurs as it did in an all-too-sincere sympathy for a people slated for death.

In the end, every modern theory of politics must face the problem of violence, or, in short, stipulate how people may be both free and safe at the same time. And without exception all such theories put forth some sort of politics, some configuration, balance, concentration, distribution, or redistribution of forces, as the solution. Yet, such flexible repackaging only appears to bring back the original problem in myriad new forms, as the ethical issues involved in the application of force never seem to get fully addressed, force being regarded, in essence, as its own remedy. Therefore, we might conclude that in imagining African American soul force, as a political entity, as a weapon of the weak, so to speak, and as a potential counterforce to white domination and black self-degradation, Du Bois held to a long and time-honored tradition. Given his ambitious goals for the achievement of black freedom, and given the dangers of any overt form of African American violence at the time that he was writing, it makes sense that he would amplify this nonviolent resource, which represented the only real force besides sheer labor power that African Americans possessed at the turn of the twentieth century, into something synonymous with their unity as a people, even at the cost of entirely underestimating just how entwined they already were in the making of whites and the making of the nation.

Conceived of as a relatively unified group sharing an ethos, African Americans could be called upon to act in concert, organize themselves around conceptions of group interest, husband their collective powers for the long-haul struggle against racism, equate resistance with dignity and with the proudest history of the group, and regard their expression—something no power could prevent—as a prime evidence of their willingness to fight back, especially at those times when more physical battles held out little hope for victory. They could even be asked to go to war, as the otherwise nonviolent but also pragmatic Du Bois encouraged them to do on two occasions. They could be bound to a sense of group loyalty, expected to disdain acts of group betrayal, and asked to bend the knee to leaders who, for the most part, possessed very little real power, save their symbolic hold over those portions of the black population that acknowledged them. Yet, as part of a unified group with a common destiny they might conceive of this submission to the supposedly more modernistic and better-equipped members of the group as an important gesture in cultivating the image of themselves as an emerging power on the American scene—and thus as true descendants of the slaves who transformed suffering into beauty by singing sorrow songs to protest slavery, who organized churches to proclaim their value in the eyes of God, and who seized the opportunity to rush to the Union lines during the Civil War, not to run away from bondage, but to conduct a strike against it. And to this bracing view of the past, Du Bois adds the confidence-enhancing future projection of African Americans as the hope of the nation, as the only real hope, in fact, that an element of humanity and originality might soften the ultimately cruel, cold, and narrowly materialistic emphasis on markets and technology that had made the country, indeed the West, powerful and notable but not yet great in the history of civilizations.

So what remains missing from this empowering picture, whose goad to creative action against racism remains so forcefully with us? I am reminded in my studies of the life and philosophy of the Indian leader and philosopher Mohandas K. Gandhi of the special and suggestive value that he placed on the untouchable, the lowest caste of his country, and the peasant. In each case, Gandhi found a potential for strength, based in a simple but powerful self-reliance, the lowliest of conditions. Without going into a long explanation of Gandhi's thought, I would just say that he valued these groups in part because they lived on so little, and thus stood a much better chance than their rulers, who surrounded themselves with things in order to reflect, announce, and guarantee their superior status, of coming into contact with their deepest, most courageous, and most powerful selves. And if they did achieve such a powerful awareness of selfhood, they did not do so by acknowledging or developing a common culture, but as individuals who had for their own reasons decided to pursue truth, but with no high priests or talented classes above them to tell them the meaning of this many-sided concept. Therefore, without proselytizing for Gandhian values, I would point out by way of contrast to Du Bois, that he found a way to value the lowliest, least powerful, one might say most "folkish" people in their lowly state, not in their guise as strivers for more power, more wealth, more modernity, essentially for something that other people possess in greater quantity than they do. In Gandhi's rendering, the peasant had a superior access to something that everyone should want, and that potentially everyone could get, so long as they held to a genuine pursuit of their deepest being.

Again, let me emphasize that I am not trying to put forward what Du Bois should have said, but what remains missing for me in the paradigm that comes down to us from him. In essence, it misses an opportunity to put the slave forward as an exemplar and as a point of criticism for the aspects of American society that, I think, Du Bois deeply disliked. Throughout his varied career, Du Bois carried on a constant criticism of American mammonism, of the tendency of the American Dream to encourage an ultimately craven glorification of wealth, power, and status seemingly without bounds. Gandhi considered such a pursuit deeply enervating, and our current culture of fear and violence speaks volumes to the basic truth of his perspective, whatever we might think of fasting, spinning one's own cloth, battling sexual temptation, or any of the actions Gandhi took in order to fashion himself an exemplar of the warrior-like courage that he regarded as every man and woman's truest, if most expensively won, inheritance. As it runs in pursuit of strength through the acquisition of material power, American culture dashes headlong in fearful retreat from the despised and pitied image of the nameless, vulnerable, used, abused, and excluded slave, whose condition inevitably haunts the seemingly magic notion of an infinite rise. Of course, those who rise infinitely may also fall into untold depths. A large part of our race problem inheres in the need to deny this negative possibility by ignoring or displacing the element of chaos and human disregard at the bottom of our most distinctive and abiding national commitments. Like Jay Gatsby, we seek the green light in part by blindsiding the blood-colored red one that that inevitably frames its meaning.

In his own way, Du Bois also pursued the green light, though he did not, like Gatsby, entirely ignore the red. Still, Du Bois needed to conceive of the slave, and of his segregated and much abused descendants, ultimately as contenders for power in order to imagine them achieving a place of honor and dignity in American society. He found little to value in the slaves' vulnerability, or in the fact that they lived on so little. Yet, more than resistance, the humble facts of dependence and death stand out most prominently in every enslaved, oppressed, or disinherited life, just as they ultimately bring low even the most powerful among us. The sincere admission of vulnerability stands behind the deepest human strength. In some ways, Du Bois acknowledges this, but if he had done so more explicitly and more completely, he might have arrived at an even more trenchant criticism of the American on one side and appreciation of the Negro on other—the two souls that remain so suggestively separated, and yet linked, in his famous concept of double consciousness. That Du Bois succeeded so well, that his hammer blows landed with such lasting force is, like all strong inheritances, a mixed blessing for us in the end. Like the words of all strong poets, his require significant recasting in order to be most fully received. Du Bois gave the potential of the slave and the racially oppressed its first truly modern articulation. It is up to us to recast his vision into more usable terms.

Notes on Escape

Of the various modes of African American resistance, escape bears the most obvious burden of contradiction. For those who regard direct assault on an oppressor as the preferred model for liberatory struggle, the notion of flight must certainly appear paltry, or even cowardly, although it has allowed African Americans constantly to "live and fight another day." Shot through with connotations of surrender and betrayal, escape nevertheless shares with the most murderous forms of resistance an insistence on making the oppressor disappear. In this way, it appears as uncompromising as revolution, but without the will to active destruction. And like revolution, escape looks forward to the construction of an entirely new state of affairs. Yet, it constantly peers backward for definition. A child of negation, it returns, sometimes tragically, to its point of origin.

Regarded as a framework of interpretation and of desire, rather than simply as an act, escape expresses the deepest wish of the slave and the oppressed for a radically different life. In this connection, it may serve as the expression of a utopian urge even when the new state of affairs to which it aspires remains only dimly sketched. Of course, one need not suffer to possess such wishes. As the philosopher Ernst Bloch asserts in *The Principle of Hope*, perhaps at the risk of overapplying his principle, the desire for a better world seems implicit in a wide range of human creative endeavor, from politics, to scientific invention, to architecture, which hinge on the faith-laden ability to apprehend appearance not just in terms of what it is but what it can be. From this viewpoint, therefore, a utopian drive may join the dreamer, the inventor, the writer, the builder, the rogue, and the slave who yearns for escape. All wish to improve existence by making it something other, and thus, in a sense, more like them in reflecting their unattained and perhaps unattainable aspirations.

Yet, it remains important to emphasize, to borrow from the nomenclature of Kenneth Burke, that escape also qualifies as a Frame of Rejection. Like the literary modes that Burke places under this label, such as burlesque, satire, and the grotesque, which express objection, complaint, or protest, escape retains an essentially negative character. Still, despite its negative character, it may, like other modes of rejection, provide a powerful form of comfort and a sense of integrity in the face of misfortune. This may especially appear the case among black Americans, where hopes for a better life in heaven, where slave masters may not enter, or in the North, in Africa, or in a transformed and truly democratic America, have often proved sustaining beyond all possibility of actual attainment. Typically, black Americans have expressed such wishes in the form of metaphors that encapsulate the often various connotations of escape, such as "flight," or the "underground," or by imagining the meaning of their history of exile and suffering through the biblical story of Exodus. Such figural expressions of escape bring together its many opposing meanings, including realism and otherworldliness, disengagement and confrontation, loyalty and betrayal, agency and surrender. The relationship between escape and resistance in the African American tradition only reveals itself through such complex refractions. They will thus provide the main focus of this chapter.

In its narrowest connotation, the theme of escape brings to mind individual attempts to evade specific oppressive conditions such as the common image of fugitive slaves escaping onrushing canine pursuers, or, perhaps more colorfully, Morgan Freeman, as the inmate Ellis "Red" Redding, tunneling his way out of prison behind his spoon-wielding buddy, the white trickster Andy Dufresne in the movie *The Shawshank Redemption*. Such representations depict escape in its least complex and most unobjectionable guise, as an attempt by the powerless person to avoid oppressive force by the most expedient means. Yet, even here, both hard-nosed realists and fans of narrative complexity might object to the melodramatic framework that most often informs the telling of such stories, which generally reduce many-sided issues to monolithic accounts of good and evil aimed more at commanding political emotions than at capturing intellectual truths. Nearly everyone familiar with black American history has encountered some version of this tendency, which places flight on a linear trajectory toward freedom.

Although some texts within the black American tradition testify to the fraught and sometimes tragic dimensions of escape, the interpretive center of gravity remains distinctly within the assumption of progressive "from / to" historical trajectory that begins in slavery and points toward a better, if not idyllic, condition to be achieved sometime in the future. Tales of escape have generally served both as moments within this larger trajectory and as signs that the hope-filled resolution may yet arrive, even after many trials and setbacks. Such a point of view informs most books that attempt comprehensively to provide an overall account of black American history, from John Hope Franklin's *From Slavery to Freedom* to Nell Painter's *Creating African Americans*. Even those who emphasize the difficulty of achieving this grand design, perhaps in the spirit of August Meier's title *From Plantation to*

Ghetto, or who doubt its efficacy altogether, tend to employ it as the main reference point for their protest against the continuing power of racism.

From the slave narratives to stories of rising from the modern black ghetto, stories of escape have also served as evidence of the willingness of African Americans to resist their oppressive condition, and thereby to occupy the position of fully free modern subjects. Although this case has sometimes justified the idea of ruggedly independent black Americans leaving the United States for Africa or other foreign lands, it has most often buttressed their rightful claim to full equality within American society, which has always prided itself on the supposedly resistant values of its citizens. In this guise, stories of African American resistance through escape have generally served the effort to write their history into the larger myth of America, as one more episode of American progress. For this bit of delicate work the evasive quality of escape has generally served well in efforts to cast black Americans as resistant yet peaceful petitioners for acceptance as full members of the nation. As many critics and historians have pointed out, for example, the slave narratives generally played up the sympathetic characteristics of slaves in implicitly making this case. Their popularity among northern white readers had a great deal to do with the way they confirmed convictions not only concerning the evil of slavery but also regarding some aspects of the American myth, which hinged on notions of opportunity, even for the most deprived, and on the putatively universal appeal of liberty. In putting their lives on the line for freedom, and in fashioning written records of their exploits, the authors of the slave narratives attempted to fit the black American story into this mold.

The fit proved less than perfect, as the effort to compile evidence of black American resistance gave ample testament to the sway of the opposite argument within the American racial imagination. This case holds that African Americans have not resisted nearly enough, that their history of enslavement has made them presumptive submitters who must prove their resistant credentials. In its most forgiving version, this thought appears as Robert Park's condescending and sympathy-laced characterization of blacks as the "Lady of the Races." In its most unforgiving form, it depicts the black American history of slavery, segregation, and other forms of victimhood as the predictable fate of a submissive, and therefore un-American, people. Usually such claims go beyond the political realm to matters of culture, or resistance to nature. In the racist imagination, claims of unforgivable submission may encompass such matters as appetite, sloth, sex, or the desire to commit violence, especially racial violence. Racist concerns of this sort most often accompany the use of power against black Americans or justify indifference to their plight. Within the larger effort to disprove such assertions, stories of escape, and the desire to escape, from bondage, poverty, social proscription, even blackness itself, have played a central role.

Further complicating the irony embedded in the tendency to view black Americans within a submissive framework, Americans have from the inception of the republic generally regarded slavery, and the African American condition in general, as the symbolic opposite of freedom—or in other words, as the defining antithesis of their own condition, and thus as the circumstance that they ought to resist at all cost. To put the matter somewhat starkly, Americans have built a collective identity as a free nation in part on a symbolic resistance not only to the condition of the most unfree people in their midst, but also to the characteristics that have marked them as a distinct group. Oddly, even as the American rhetoric of independence, rebellion, rejection of the past, dominance of nature, and many other categories has suggested resistance to black Americans as a requirement for full inclusion, American society has placed innumerable barriers in the way of their progress, partly to exclude them for having been so radically excluded. Of course, such resistance has continually re-created the necessary condition for the long tradition of black American sacrifice in the name of freedom and recognition even as it has given rise to an interminable concern with whether the country can ever live down, or escape, its own past. In resisting mightily the terms of their oppression, black Americans have generally answered this question in the affirmative even as their struggle has reminded other Americans of the continuing grip of a seemingly inescapable history. Thus, even in petitioning for recognition, black Americans have continually set themselves apart by reminding other Americans of a legacy whose full reality many have staked themselves on denying. Yet, in another way, resistance makes black Americans into quintessential representatives of the best values of the nation, endlessly praised for their inspiring resilience and for their ability to maintain hope in seemingly hopeless situations.

No wonder then that escape, both as action and desire, appears the most inescapable theme of African American history and artistic expression. Broadly considered, the large narrative structure of African American history begins with a forced exile from Africa and proceeds through several major escapes, first from slavery and then from the South in two major northward migrations precipitated by the world wars. The civil rights struggle might be considered yet another kind of escape, this time from legal segregation. Today, some observers praise the arrival of a post-racial era, or a transcendence of race altogether. Such an optimistic account of our own time may well arise from the desire to complete a history of escapes with the sense of an ending, although it does so while toying with uncomfortable implications of erasure. As the large structure of African American history foregrounds exit, many of its smaller events and phenomena reverberate this theme: Symbolic or actual returns to Africa; the establishment of black towns and imaginary black worlds; expatriatism; passing for white; multiracialism; intermarriage; and class mobility have all at various points held out for African Americans the possibility of evading the gravitational pull of race, either by leaving the category entirely behind or, perhaps more ironically, through pragmatic or ecstatic embrace.

At times, black Americans have sought escape in response to extraordinary opportunities, like those of the 1920s, when the North beckoned with economic promise, but they have most commonly gravitated to this idea in the darkest times, such as the 1850s or the 1890s, when white Americans generally closed their ears to ideas of racial progress, or even worse, conducted overtly violent racist campaigns to preserve slavery or to keep "niggers" in their place. In other words, exit has appealed most to African Americans when events have dictated most insistently that they face the unique "no exit" character of their condition. During one such difficult period, the "Southern Colored Woman" of Hamilton Holt's turn-of-the-twentieth-century collection *The Life Stories of Undistinguished Americans* (1906) expressed the seeming inescapability of the African American circumstance well when she addressed Lee Chew, a Chinese immigrant, who responded to white racism by threatening to take his money with him back to China: "Happy Chinaman! Fortunate Lee Chew!" the Southern Colored Woman retorted. "You can go back to your village and enjoy your money. [America] is my village, my home, yet am I an outcast." In the same period, the African American public intellectual Kelly Miller struck a similar, though more philosophical, note when he observed that American racial realities yielded only three options to the descendants of slaves: "Get out, get white, or get along." With the first two utterly out of the question, he concluded, black Americans must embrace the last, however much such a posture might offend the race pride of fighters and idealists within the group.

In advising his brethren to approach pragmatically their social and cultural ills, Miller responded not only to the political aspects of African American oppression in his own time, but also to the perennial "no exit" character of American racial standards, which insist on an absolute line of demarcation between black and white. Under this rule, whose final demise some current observers view in the offing, blackness represents a heritable stain of such power that it can spoil the supposed purity of whiteness with only the smallest admixture. Whether depicted as an internal condition of the blood or soul, or as an external physical mark, the sign of blackness in American culture has historically indicated an absolute divide between whole states of being. As a "master" social status, blackness has tended to override the perception of other indications of social distinction, including class, ethnicity, and, to a certain extent, even gender. Lumped together into a single social category, despite their many differences, African Americans have sometimes felt trapped, as Ralph Ellison's Invisible Man (IM) observes, by a "peculiar disposition of the eyes of those with whom [they] come into contact." Describing his condition as "one of invisibility," he compares himself to "bodiless heads you see sometimes in circus sideshows" and to the situation of one surrounded by mirrors of hard, distorting glass. "When they approach me," he says, "they see only my surroundings, themselves, or figments of their imagination—indeed, everything and anything except me."

In this moment, when he testifies to the power of the white gaze, the invisible man may well join Jean-Paul Sartre's character Garcin of the play *No Exit* in proclaiming that "Hell is—other people." A prisoner within the iron cage of racism throughout his life, and tempted by hard experience to prefer the bad faith of victimhood to the anguish and responsibility of freedom, the narrator explains in the prologue to *Invisible Man* why his escape into an underground hole, away from the distorting eyes of his oppressors, has effected self-confrontation and transformation rather than decline and death. To account for this outcome, he constructs his life story as the tragicomic tale of a man who used oppression and other externally imposed circumstances as excuses to avoid the burden of an authentic life, which requires every individual to regard his actions as essentially his own. Having run a gauntlet of available identities for a black man in his time—from southern black college student, to industrial worker, to community activist, to hustler and pimp—he has exhausted all options for social and personal recognition just at the point in the novel when a group of white thugs, hard at work defending the borderlands of white America from rioting Harlemites, chases him into a manhole, and into a timeless, dark underworld where he must face himself honestly or die. Confronted with a clear choice between life and death, self-recognition or chaos, and electing to live, he must for the first time, and with great pain, regard his whole life to that point as a series of free choices, and himself, for better and for worse, as the product of those decisions. From this tough standpoint, he reconstructs the story of his life.

Looking forward, and taking his new life philosophy to its logical end, he regards himself as the agent of his own creation within the context of a chaotic and often hostile universe. Looking backward, he realizes that many black

Americans before him, and some of the characters in his own life, like his grandfather, the sharecropper Jim Trueblood, and the hipster Peter Wheatstraw, have come to similar conclusions. Having made the tough choice to accept the rigors of their essential human freedom, they do more than to say "no" to the white gaze. By accepting their essential freedom, even under oppression, they say "yes" to life. Thus linked to a tradition of black self-affirmation, IM proclaims the principle of liberty and democracy for all. His acceptance of his own freedom, his "yes" to life, requires him to affirm the liberty and potential of all other individuals as a condition for his own. At the same time, he declares himself responsible to act in accordance with this principle. Transformed from the vulnerable and self-deceiving IM that the white gaze defines, he becomes invisible in a second sense, one that allows him to embrace his concealment. Now with new protection from outside perceptions, he promises to end his "overdone" hibernation, emerge from the underground, and discover what "responsible social role" he might play. Yet, he remains "conflicted" and ever mindful of the chaos against which any idea of living must conceive its pattern. He remains, quite properly, unwilling to say precisely what he will do next.

With the possible exception of Thoreau's *Walden*, American arts and letters can claim no greater elucidation of the democratic potential inherent in escape than *Invisible Man*. Yet, the novel achieves its purpose by running against the general obsession with worlds "elsewhere" and vantage points beyond society that many regard as important distinguishing characteristics of American literature and culture. Rather than a place of final rest or fulfillment, the underground in *Invisible Man* represents a territory of inner retreat, self-confrontation, trial, renewal, and preparation for a return, perhaps an eternal creative return, to a hostile society. Based heavily on the values of action and voice, the novel succeeds as a statement on the potential of escape largely because it arrays so much against the idea of a comfortable and stable outside. In addition, *Invisible Man* focuses on the black condition, the only symbolically inescapable circumstance in American life, as a foil for its concern with escape. Because it locates a space of freedom within the confines of black American life, a kind of built-in escape that nonetheless augurs democratic involvement, *Invisible Man* affirms the American Dream of arrival in a bounteous land located beyond quotidian cares and worries as it shifts the register of hope to a territory at once more tragic and more uplifting.

In evoking the image of the underground, *Invisible Man* does not so much invent a new metaphor as it mines an important trope within black American memory, where the idea of escaping within the neighborhood, so to speak, or near family and friends, sometimes took precedence over more common and dramatic renderings of flight across a border into a realm of unambiguous freedom. In contrast to this more common notion, the idea of the underground appears to hold out for a space of refuge within the borderlands of slavery that nonetheless preserves the potential of aid and comfort from one's own on familiar terrain, so long as one can remain unseen and unheard by whites. Although a bit colder, and perhaps more realistic, in its slave renderings than the "warm" and well-lit subterranean retreat of Ellison's invisible protagonist, the underground metaphor derived its power from its assertion of a hidden black potential that could coincide with the worst oppression and yet, at the same time, live outside of it. In this way, it signified the unrecognized agency of the millions of African Americans who never tried to escape, or never could. Even if no clear promised land existed, it seemed to imply, the sheer infinity of the wilderness, both within and without, offered up literal and metaphorical possibilities that the masters could not circumscribe.

In *Strategies for Survival: Recollections of Bondage in Antebellum Virginia* (2009), a book based on a treasure trove of WPA interviews of ex-slaves completed by black interviewees during the 1930s, historian William Dusinberre quotes ex-slave Charles Grandy, who recollects John Salley, "a slave . . . dat runned away. He runned away and didn' never come back. Didn' go no place neither. Stayed right roun' de plantation. Use to come in at night an' steal hawgs an' chickens fer food. Dat ole man died in de woods. Never did come out." Another ex-slave recalls an encounter with a member of the storied maroon colony in the Dismal Swamp, located between Virginia and North Carolina, where fugitives lived in underground shelters to evade slave catchers: "De runaway slave used to come out and beg us for food. At fust we was scared to deaf of 'em and jes' fly, but after while we used to steal bred an' fresh meat an' give to 'em. But dey never would let you foller 'em. Dey hide in Dismal Swamp in holes in de groun' so hidden dey stay dere years an' white folks, dogs, or nothin' else could fine 'em." In this account, as in Ellison's classic, invisibility imbues vulnerability with a fearful, almost magical, power. Apparently, even as they represented a certain fierce independence, black maroons from the swamplands could strike fear even into the hearts of slaves, who may have been taken aback by the association of these fugitives with the unknown and the unseen, or with their own yearning for freedom, perhaps projected backward into an African past as opposed to an American future. Yet, so long as it remained alive in group memory, the idea of a hidden world of blackness—not so much free as unfettered, not so much resistant as inaccessible to power—could serve not only as a metaphor of possibility for slaves but also as an enduring image of hope for black Americans after emancipation, where stories of flying across Jordan, escaping or migrating to the North, or leaving American shores altogether, have never quite encompassed the odd braiding of freedom and unfreedom that has characterized the black American condition from the coming of the Union troops to the inauguration of the first black president.

As Henry Louis Gates Jr. has pointed out most prominently, the anomalous fate of black Americans within American culture has given rise to a peculiar affection for rhetorical figures that reverse expected relationships between high and low, inside and outside, sacred and profane. In locating a potential place of redemption or independence in a subterranean location beyond the reach of society, the underground metaphor follows this pattern, as does the peculiar density of positive meaning around the term "down" in black American culture. In "Dis and Dat: Dialect and Descent," Gates focuses specifically on religious discourse, as in the songs "Go Down Moses," "Down in the Valley," or "Down by the Riverside" to assert the term "down" as the location for the enactment of "primal tragic action, where fate and will can meet." "Down," Gates asserts, "is the Afro-American 'Fourth Stage,' that place where Yahweh told Moses exactly what to say to old Pharaoh, 'way down in Egypt Land,' to 'let my people go.'" A speaker of modern black American slang might say in playful response that Moses was "down" with God, or "down" with the cause of his people.

Today, the religious implications of the term "down" have given way to an explosion of secular, and decidedly un-tragic, associations, which nevertheless carry on the idea of a place below the social radar where the work of the spirit takes place. In this connection "down" may mean sharing a secret or intimacy with someone, knowing a rare hidden truth, or being "in the groove," as in getting "down" like James Brown, who reminds us in "Funky Good Time" that "in order for me to get down, I've got to get in [the key of] D." In another famous song, the group Cool and the Gang urges dancers to "get down on it" after repeating several times the vague but irresistible question "What you wanna do? Do you want to get down?" Parliament Funkadelic, in another funk anthem, cites both sexual and jazz-oriented notions of the downbeat, in encouraging all lovers of life to "get up on the downstroke," or to go underwater and do the "Aquaboogie," which allows one miraculously "to dance underwater and not get wet." In an even more hopeful register, Parliament announces in "One Nation under a Groove" the possibility of an unstoppable funk nation, or anti-nation—presumably an alternative to racial, religious, or other essentialist myths of national origin—made up of citizens who are perpetually "gettin' down just for the funk of it," and who in mocking reference to the biblically ensured pledge at the inception of all legal testimony that aligns perjury with sin "promise to funk, the whole funk, and nothin' but the funk."

Although well aware of the wider and more playful signifyin' diffusion of the term "down," Gates confines his analysis in "Dis and Dat" to more solemn concerns with questions of sin and redemption. Citing the much quoted spiritual refrain "Went down to the rocks to hide my face, / The rocks cried out no hiding place," Gates associates this use of the term "down" with a place of confrontation "within the spirit of the soul, of the poet with the ineffable." The sinner who seeks to flee the implications of his sin by refusing to face God may find that in the very place refuge, where God seems most remote, even the cold and inanimate rocks will, like the boxer Joe Louis, remind the feckless evader that "you can run but you can't hide." One might say that here God is the ultimate slave catcher because He captures and manumits in the same gesture both slaves and masters alike. As Gates elucidates the more narrowly Christian meaning of a black American encounter with talking rocks, which suggest to him the special priority of the spoken over the written word, he asserts that the signifyin' range of the term "down" extends backward more than forward to a barely visible lost home in Africa, now endowed with a certain spiritual mystery of primitive origins, collective unconscious, and a return to a truer and deeper selfhood. Perhaps so, but a more complete analysis might add to this range of meanings the more un-homely associations that Gates leaves out, especially those of the middle passage, where the captive Africans truly descended into a tough and transformative confrontation with the limits of culture, and slavery itself, where social death became for them permanent fact of life.

Closely related to their many uses of the term "down," black Americans have also expressed their affection for figures of reversal through metaphors of flight, or going upward, which appear with a similar cultural density as those expressing descent or downward states of being. Although metaphors of flight generally involve a leap toward a qualitatively different, and usually better, state of being, they often appear alongside various references to downward movement of some sort, especially in the common linkage of freedom with death. Such balanced or countervailing metaphors may also describe the odd twists of the inner life, as in the spiritual "Nobody Knows the Trouble I've Seen," where a beautiful description of life's sweetness, even in slavery, gives way to an equally compelling acknowledgment of an ever-present sadness.

> One morning I was walking down
> I saw some berries hanging down
> I pick de berry and I suck the juice,
> Just as sweet as honey in the comb.

Sometimes I'm up, sometimes I'm down
Sometimes I'm almost on the groun'.

In the spiritual "Lay This Body Down," the simultaneous upward and downward movement of life and death, bondage and escape, repeats the natural circular motion of the cosmos, where rising and setting celestial spheres provide light in darkness and darkness in light:

I walk in de moonlight,
I walk in de starlight,
To lay dis body down.
I'll walk through the graveyard,
To lay dis body down.
I'll lie in de grave and stretch out my arms;
Lay dis body down.
I go to de judgment in de
evenin' of de day,
When I lay dis body down;
And my soul and your soul
will meet in de day
When I lay dis body down.

In the spiritual "Swing Low, Sweet Chariot" the angels, who are referred to as "coming after" the believer almost like a slave patrol chasing a fugitive, must, in another figure of reversal, fly low to carry her away to heaven, which the song describes as "home" in seeming reference to the many slave songs that describe this life as a wilderness or a condition of exile. In "Motherless Child" a sad sentiment at the beginning of the song seems almost erased by a joyful reference to flying at the end: "Sometimes I feel like/A eagle in the air. . . . Spread my wings an'/Fly, fly, fly. Like "Nobody Knows the

Trouble I've Seen," this song emphasizes the alternation of moods within the inner depths, but this time lifted up by fellowship with God. Another slave song, reflecting a thought similar to the aforementioned "No Hiding Place," where "going down" corresponds with the effort of the sinner to hide his face from God, tempers the image of flight with the idea of having two sets of wings that carry out opposing tasks: "I've got two wings for to veil my face/I've got two wings for to fly away."

As with the term "down," modern black American uses of flight imagery repeat some of the older, more solemn, religious concerns of the slave songs, but also add a more playful dimension. Aficionados of urban black slang might make this point in noting the common use of the word "fly" as a synonym for "attractive," as in "That's a fly hat you're wearing," or in the occasional references in rap songs to "fly girls" or "fly guys" out on the town. Followers of popular culture might find this theme reflected in such names as Superfly, a drug dealer whose death-defying grasp of the cruel street game allowed him to defy the white mob; Charlie "Bird" Parker, a jazzman whose saxophone seemed to soar in an otherworldly manner above the rest; or Air Jordan, a basketball player of such surpassing ability that his name not only signifies flight but also the gravity-defying element in which it takes place. Historians of the twentieth century may recall the Garveyite aviator Hubert Fauntleroy Julian, the "Black Eagle of Harlem," also known, perhaps somewhat less spectacularly, as the "Negro Lindbergh" for making a transatlantic flight in 1931. The first black person to earn a flying license in the United States, Julian gained Ethiopian citizenship in 1930 when he parachuted to the feet of Emperor Haile Selassie during an aerial display featuring the modernistic Negro's grasp of martial technology—a theme repeated by the legend of the

Tuskegee airmen, but along integrationist lines. Unfortunately, Julian's leap foreshadowed his fate much better than his adroit landing. He lost his much-prized Ethiopian citizenship in the same year that he received it when he crashed one of the Emperor's most coveted airplanes in front of an international audience, giving the traditional black American theme of flight's downward accent a somewhat comical illustration.

During the World War II era, Lionel Hampton's fast-paced jazz-vibraphone hit "Flying Home" offered yet another version of the flight theme in black American culture. According to Hampton, the catchy refrain of "Flying Home" had its origin in his own fear of flying, as he hummed it repeatedly whenever he entered an airplane. In the early part of her career, jazz singer Ella Fitzgerald made a famous "scat" version of Hampton's song. Late in life, she put words to it that combined themes of freedom, flight, death, and self-possession in a fashion that appears almost directly to arise from the spirituals even as she testifies to the somewhat mystical and wonderful correspondence of nature and technology:

> And now the sun is beginning to rise,
> It's like looking down on Paradise,
> There's a ball of fire that's burning,
> Giving life
>
> And we are flying home,
> I feel the freedom in my soul,
> Flying home at last;
> Flying home,
> I've got the freedom in my soul,
> And it's four in the morning,

> My world is calling,
> Speeding through the universe tonight. ("Flying Home,"
> Ella Fitzgerald)

In these lyrics, Fitzgerald evokes a peak experience not only of flying high, but of being high, a transportation away from the self and in another sense a return to it, of being grounded by the intoxicating combination of altitude and speed.

Afterword

GEORGE B. HUTCHINSON

When Jeffrey Ferguson passed away in March 2018, at a tragically young age after living with cancer for several years, he was working on *Race and the Rhetoric of Resistance*, a highly original project prefigured by important essays in the journals *Raritan*, *Daedalus*, and *Amerikastudien*. The essays collected here form a coherent argument, overlapping but never repetitive. Together they amount to a provocative, complex, and subtle critique of pervasive rhetorical reflexes in American and African American Studies. As the foreword to this book points out, the author is best known for his excellent book on George Schuyler published by Yale University Press, and one can sense here the ironic and iconoclastic intelligence featured in that book—which is not to say that Ferguson shares Schuyler's politics or at times seemingly nihilistic streak, but that he is keen to descry self-contradiction, group narcissism, and disavowed hypocrisy on all sides of American racial melodrama. Although the chapters occasionally refer to events coincident with the time of their publication, particularly Obama's presidential run, they are never period pieces, and the argument is as relevant today as ever. Indeed, it is likely to remain relevant for some time to come, for it addresses perdurable patterns of American intellectual culture.

The book begins, appropriately, with "Race and the Rhetoric of Resistance," a rich, wide-ranging, and eloquently written essay that targets what must surely be the strongest theme in African American Studies, as well as cultural studies generally. Ferguson illuminates how a tendency to posit resistance as the only authentic form of blackness becomes a self-perpetuating pattern that obscures other powerful and necessary aspects of African American expression.

He is surely right that suffering and resistance are the "two basic stories" of the discourse on African Americans. "Race," Ferguson points out, "has stood out for the extreme way that it manifests both the persistence of suffering and the great hope that by fighting against it human beings might deliver themselves from its grasp." Ferguson draws effortlessly from a wide range of texts and foundational secondary studies; his generalizations are apt and well supported, often by touchstones many readers will recognize even if they've never read them. One needn't be a specialist to follow the argument. The emphasis on "resistance," he points out, has fed off of and helped perpetuate an emphasis on "race melodrama," victimization and heroic resistance, outer-directed rebellion more than inner experience, and finally a drama of *ressentiment* now felt on both "sides" of the color line. "For the skeptic," Ferguson writes, "the utter dominance of the theme of resistance in the current discourse on black Americans should evoke some suspicion." Indeed, that theme is so dominant that many readers are likely to respond, immediately, that *of course* that's what African American culture is about; what else could it be—passivity and acceptance of the status quo?

As Ferguson points out, mainstream recognition of the very humanity of African Americans has in part been based on their resistance to subjugation, in line with Enlightenment notions of the human. However, Ferguson argues, while this framework emphasizes central features of African

American experience and expression ("bravery, sacrifice, and ideas of dignity based on these"), "it tends to subsume such other themes as pleasure, artistic invention, religious belief, and issues of interracial and intraracial solidarity into a narrow set of dualities concerning submission and defiance."

There are, of course, reasons for connecting blackness with resistance, and the pattern emerged early. Ferguson traces some of that history, featuring particularly the sentimental and melodramatic conventions we find in *Uncle Tom's Cabin*. Ferguson also allows that even "race melodrama" has had positive effects. Nonetheless, its dominance has left too much out of our ken that is also important to African American culture and experience. "The resistance framework obscures as much as it clarifies." It ignores the fact that for people in situations of extreme suffering, an ethics of care for one another is often more important, even to maintaining one's own sense of humanity, than resistance—a point made by Tzvetan Todorov's *Facing the Extreme*, which dealt with the Holocaust.

Ferguson's eye for performative contradictions and irony is relentless. The association of blackness with breaking boundaries around race while at the same time maintaining group integrity, he points out, requires that the boundaries retain their force—something some authors, such as Richard Wright, fully recognized, although the point is rarely mentioned in scholarship on his work. The first step to getting out of a vicious cycle is to recognize it as one. Ferguson does not prescribe a way out, but forces us to attend to other options. African Americans have other patterns of finding or making meaning in life than suffering and resistance, and these patterns deserve more attention than they have received.

Subsequent chapters build on the point of view epitomized by the first. Thus "Freedom, Equality, Race" addresses the three terms that in many ways define the distinctive qualities of American social history. Once again, Ferguson is keenly attuned to the contradictions in American ideology—how the discourses of race and of freedom developed simultaneously in the Enlightenment and, as Edmund Morgan has shown in a classic historical study, imprinted the foundations of American identity. The two concepts did not merely coincide; the white American ideal of "freedom" depended on the existence of slavery.

Similarly, the discourse of equality helped nurture in white Americans a kind of paranoia—the fear of being "losers," unequal in fact if not in formal political status. Thus the formal status of blacks as unequal buttressed their sense of being free citizens of the republic—the "psychological wage" Du Bois famously identified. Ferguson then finishes with the paradox that, as some of the formal props of racial inequality have been dismantled and the black middle class has grown (indicating racial "progress"), the discursive boundary of race has been reproduced as a necessary "mode of classification" to keep the progress coming. Any hope for a "raceless" future seems a naïve (at best) threat to the equality sought. The "party of hope" and the "party of memory" remain locked in a wrestling match with no evident solution, for race has marked the very principles that we regard as raceless, such as freedom and equality. Once again, Ferguson does not presume to offer a solution but instead concludes that "a new narrative" is needed. This is a challenge deserving further investigation, for narrative competes with the necessarily bifurcating processes of human cognition in making sense of experience, linking different things together through story rather than logical operations, shaping our experience of time and identity.

"A Blue Note on Black American Literary Criticism and the Blues," like the chapter on the "rhetoric of resistance," critiques a pervasive strain in African Americanist literary criticism, the idealization of the blues as the foundation of black intellectual production, a vernacular locus of authentic, distinctively black, resistance. This may be less pervasive today than it was in the late twentieth century and early in this one, but it has never really been critiqued as comprehensively and knowledgeably as it is in this essay. Ferguson draws on a wealth of knowledge about the blues, studies of blues, and black literary theory to show how unlikely is the foundation on which soi-disant "blues critics" base their arguments. They seem, he suggests, to be exploiting a prestige conferred on the blues through its commercial resurgence at various moments and the myths that grew up around it in the process—a great irony, indeed. Here again we find the essentially satirical, ironic imagination of the author, conveyed, however, with great subtlety and erudition. "Despite Baraka's claims for the separateness of black culture," he points out, "his *Blues People* corresponds directly with the early days of the 1960s folk music movement, which spurred a renewed interest in the blues among young people across the United States. In other words, literary critics seem to see the greatest possibilities for the blues at the very times when everybody else does." Ferguson goes on to detail how important commercialization was to the growth of the form, the diversity of its subject matter and tone, and melding of influences from a wide variety of styles. Above all, blues "makes its greatest mark for its apolitical and anti-resistant posture." It "emphasizes most the internal resources of the individual to affirm life, even in the darkest times"—a point that echoes and reinforces from a new direction a central point of the first chapter of this book. At the conclusion of the essay, Ferguson proceeds to the equally valuable point that "the entire idea of grounding a literary tradition at all might be regarded as an ideological vestige of a bygone era" and, in fact, "we do not need the idea of a literary tradition with a capital *T*."

In "Of Mr. W.E.B. Du Bois and Others," Ferguson addresses yet another foundational strain in African American Studies—the view of Du Bois as one of the principal "sources for conceiving of African American life as a resistant and embattled condition" that will find its solution in a "battle-ready, self-recognizing, and self-transcending people." Indeed, this notion one might point to as virtually the reason-for-being of Africana Studies departments and programs in the United States. Ferguson identifies a fivefold argument, articulated in *The Souls of Black Folk*, for the direction that black cultural politics must take at the battlefront of freedom, in which a group ethos, epitomized and articulated by a Talented Tenth elite, shall batter down the walls of Jericho. Ferguson finds that what is missing in Du Bois's powerful formulation is what Gandhi put forward in the potential for a different sort of strength he saw in the lowest of the low—not a striving for power and wealth but for something else "that everyone should want, and that potentially everyone could get, so long as they held to a genuine pursuit of their deepest being."

This is a more contemplative form of life than the one for which Du Bois argued. The effect of Ferguson's argument is to show how much Du Bois had in common with his American brothers and sisters across the color line. "As it runs in pursuit of strength through the acquisition of material power, American culture dashes headlong in fearful retreat from the despised and pitied image of the nameless, vulnerable, used, abused, and excluded slave." Honor and dignity, for Du Bois, come only through external power. What is again striking here is the fit of this argument of Ferguson's with the preceding chapters. Each chapter, in fact, builds on and buttresses the others, so that this book comprises more than a collection of essays; it forms a cohesive argument with a solid structure.

Thus the final chapter draft, "Notes on Escape," approaches one of the perennial motifs of African American expression going back to slavery and the dream of flying away home. Ferguson emphasizes the utopian mode of escape, the desire for another way of life—which, as in the spirituals is not only a life free of slavery, assimilable to America's progress narrative, but a life "inaccessible to power"—a brilliant way of putting the existential, even universal reverberations of this desire. Ferguson draws nearest in this chapter to indicating the options other than "resistance" that lead out of the vicious cycles he has featured earlier in the book. This chapter draws from a wide range of African American cultural touchstones to explore all the ways in which notions of escape—flight and going underground, in particular—exemplify modes other than resistance in the common sense. "I've got the freedom in my soul," sings Ella Fitzgerald in "Flying Home" (also the title of a brilliant early story by Ralph Ellison). "My world is calling." The chapter breaks off at this point, leaving us with the inescapable pathos of knowing that Ferguson may have been facing the inescapability of departure as he wrote it, not something any of us, in the final analysis, can "resist."

Race and the Rhetoric of Resistance opens thought to a different way of thinking, maybe different, neglected narratives within African American culture responding to a complex fate. It is a genuine intervention in African American and American Studies, inherently provocative, yet advanced in a thoughtful, contemplative tone appropriate to its argument and revealing of the generous sensibility behind it. It seems to me a bravura performance on the edge of the abyss, and a gift to those who come after.

Editor's Acknowledgments

I am grateful to Micah Kleit and Nicole Solano for asking me to edit and introduce Jeffrey Ferguson's *Race and the Rhetoric of Resistance* for Rutgers University Press and to George Hutchinson for reviewing the whole text carefully and writing an afterword. Thanks to Gregory Hyman for managing production of the book's interior, to Barbara Goodhouse for copyediting the manuscript, and to Geronna Lyte for designing the cover.

"Race and the Rhetoric of Resistance" originally appeared in *Raritan*, Summer 2008, Vol. 28(1), pp. 4–32. Thanks to T. J. Jackson Lears.

"Freedom, Equality, Race" was first published in *Daedalus*, Winter 2011, Vol. 140(1), pp. 44–52. Thanks to Gerald Early and Phyllis S. Bendell.

"A Blue Note on Black American Literary Criticism and the Blues" was part of a special issue of *Amerikastudien/American Studies*, January 2010, Vol. 55(4), pp. 699–714. Thanks to Glenda R. Carpio, Udo J. Hebel, and Universitätsverlag Winter.

"Of Mr. W.E.B. Du Bois and Others" (a paper delivered on February 16, 2013, at the CUNY Graduate Center symposium "W.E.B. Du Bois, Slavery, and the Atlantic Imaginary") and "Notes on Escape" were manuscripts in the estate of Jeffrey B. Ferguson. Many thanks to Agustina Ferguson for making them available for their first publication in this volume.

Index

About the Contributors

JEFFREY B. FERGUSON (1964–2018) was Karen and Brian Conway Presidential Teaching Professor of Black Studies at Amherst College, a mythical teacher, and author of *The Sage of Sugar Hill: George S. Schuyler, Satire, and the Harlem Renaissance* (2005), *Harlem Renaissance: A Brief History with Documents* (2007), and an essay on Sinclair Lewis's *Babbitt* for *A New Literary History of America* (2009).

WERNER SOLLORS is Henry B. and Anne M. Cabot Professor of English and African American Studies, *Emeritus*, at Harvard University and author of *Amiri Baraka: The Quest for a "Populist Modernism"* (1978), *Neither Black nor White yet Both: Thematic Explorations of Interracial Literature* (1998), *The Temptation of Despair: Tales of the 1940s* (2014), and other books.

GEORGE B. HUTCHINSON is professor of English, Newton C. Farr Professor of American History and Culture, and director of the John S. Knight Institute for Writing in the Disciplines, all at Cornell University in Ithaca, New York. He is the author of numerous books, including *In Search of Nella Larsen: A Biography of the Color Line* (2006) and *Facing the Abyss: American Literature and Culture in the 1940s* (2018).